Dare to Trust Dare to Hope Again

Living with Losses of the Heart

Kari West

For Her. For God. For Real.
faithfulwoman.com

Faithful Woman is an imprint of
Cook Communications Ministries, Colorado Springs, Colorado 80918
Cook Communications, Paris, Ontario
Kingsway Communications, Eastbourne, England

DARE TO TRUST, DARE TO HOPE AGAIN

First Printing, 2001
Printed in the United States of America

1 2 3 4 5 6 7 8 9 10 Printing/Year 05 04 03 02 01

Editors: Lori Davis; Julie Smith and Craig Bubeck, Sr. Editors
Cover & Interior Design: Andrea Boven / Boven Design Studio, Inc.

Acknowledgement

With heartfelt gratitude . . .

To each woman who shared her story of loss. Thank you for opening your heart and allowing me access to your sorrow, fears, hopes, and dreams. Your transparency encourages others to believe they can and will survive life's losses, too.

To the DivorceWise survivor sisters. You are a major reason I write. Special appreciation to Becky in Georgia, whose e-mail "I'm resting in God's arms of mercy" helped me visualize this project. Also, to Maurine in Colorado, who first voiced the need for such a book as this.

To Jon, John, Cliff, Steve, and Nancy of the Hayward Writers Critique Group. Thanks for your encouragement, prayers, and input. Special appreciation to Diane Smith and Patricia Avery for reading every word in the manuscript. Your suggestions made this book broader and better than I first imagined.

To Julie Smith and Lori Davis, editors who recognize the value of this work; and to Craig Bubeck, for seeing this project through to the end.

To my husband, Richard, for believing in me and for providing the opportunity to indulge my passion for writing. Thanks for overlooking the morning coffee I neglected to make and the meals I did not cook. You are a blessing from God. I love you with all my heart.

Contents

Section 7

Daring Moments When I Face My Fears

Section 8

Decisive Moments That Fuel Change and Clarify My Perspective

Section 9

Elastic Moments for Reaching Up and Stretching Out

SECTION 10

Spirited Moments for Traveling Lighter and Trusting More

SECTION 11

Glorious Moments for Simply Celebrating Life

SECTION 12

Courageous Moments When I Risk Hoping Again

I rise early, before the sun is up;
I cry out for help
and put my hope in your words.
I stay awake through the night,
thinking about your promise.

PSALM 119:147-148

Introduction

This book is about living with life's catastrophes. It specifically addresses one area of suffering—being a victim of losses for which you were not responsible and over which you had little or no control. While its stories cover a wide range of issues, this book is not a comprehensive study of loss. It does not tell you "how to" get over loss but invites self-reflection, the deepening of faith, and the willingness to be changed forever as you dare to trust and hope again in the midst of life's uncertainties.

Life is like a page-a-day calendar. The days are limited and forever changing. Within this progressive time frame, you can step forward but you cannot move backward. The only certainties besides death and taxes are brevity, change, and loss. But life's catastrophic losses can leave you in a daze—emotionally overwhelmed, mentally confused, physically exhausted, and spiritually shaken.

Getting over a loss is never easy—whether you lose a loved one, a marriage, a home, your health, or your youth. Perhaps you are newly widowed, separated, or divorced. Perhaps you have a broken engagement or you are grieving the death of a parent, a friend, or a child. When the unexpected happens, you can lose a dream along with the will to go on. You could lose trust in God.

Loss is disorienting—whenever it happens and whatever you lose. At the very time you need your wits about you to tackle the overwhelming tasks ahead, you feel broadsided by unbearable sorrow. You ask yourself, *How do I make plans for tomorrow when I'm not sure I can get through the next minute?*

Each day your to-do list grows a lot longer and your spirit unravels a little further. Time seems warped and your calendar, out of control. You can't comprehend how you will manage a day, let alone imagine the future. You aren't even sure you will make it through the morning. You struggle to get out of bed and off to work—or you wonder how you will find a job, if you've never worked. It is an effort to dress or comb your hair. In public, you feel embarrassed that you appear a little scatterbrained. In secret, you wonder, *Am I going crazy?*

You try to make sense of things, while your heart flutters over *what might have been* and your mind ruminates about *what was*. You are perplexed with the *why me?* and the *how come now?* of what happened. Sometimes there isn't even one person you can turn to for answers. Few friends really understand, unless they have stood where you now stand. You even doubt yourself.

As you struggle to gain your footing in these seemingly endless gaps between yesterday, today, and tomorrow, you may ask, *What's the use?* Some days you sit in the darkness questioning whether you are a worthwhile human being. You feel like someone walked away with a part of you.

No wonder these dazed times that accompany a loss are such heavy times! Each day is pregnant with moments that are life-giving and life-changing. Moments to reorder priorities or to rethink the rest of your life. Moments when you are forced to go deeper in your spiritual life so that your anguish can be embraced by the *not-always- easy-to-understand* love of an *always-understanding* God. Meditational moments that give you permission *to be* still instead of *to do* more.

Maybe all you can do right now is simply to *be*.Today, you are trying to be the best person, the best parent, or the best friend you can, with what little energy and focus you have left. It's okay. Do not be afraid. The dust will settle. The children will survive. The e-mail can wait. Tomorrow you can chip away at that to-do list again.

Wherever you are in your passage through unspeakable loss,

you need to know that you are not alone in what you are experiencing. We all have days we muddle through the moments and wonder, *Now, what do I do?*

Be patient with yourself. Take time to sort through what you have lost and what you have left. Snuggle in the Father's arms of mercy. He knows the daze you are in—mentally, emotionally, spiritually, and physically. In time, clarity will replace confusion. Chaos will give way to order. You won't always be standing in the same puddle of tears or thrusting your fist at a dark sky. Coming to terms with loss takes time. You need time to integrate the loss into your life.

In the meantime, may the words in this book help you survive the moments. As you start slinging your feet off the bed and stepping into each new day on your calendar, look up and stand tall. You are worth the struggle. Soon you'll know exactly what to do next.

—*Kari West*

P.S. I know you don't believe it right now, but your life is not over yet. God still has plans for you. In Heaven's perpetual calendar, loss is but an earthly interruption. There is a future beyond grief. Someday soon you'll see.

"*For I know the plans I have for you*," declares the Lord,
"plans to prosper you and not to harm you,
plans to give you *hope* and a *future*."

JEREMIAH 29:11 NIV

Emotional Moments

Meant for Whole-Hearted Embracing

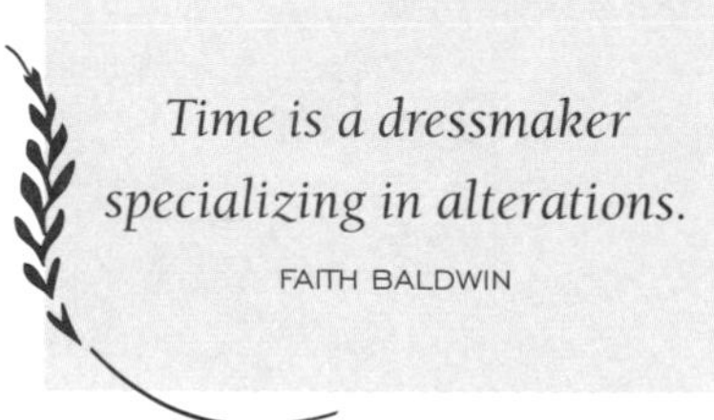

Time is a dressmaker
specializing in alterations.

FAITH BALDWIN

1. This is not how I planned my life

I am worn out from sobbing.
Every night tears drench my bed;
my pillow is wet from weeping.
My vision is blurred by grief. . . .

PSALM 6:6-7

You have lost something or someone very dear to you. The tears won't stop. The pain won't go away. Whenever loss happens and whatever you lose, unspeakable anguish becomes your constant companion.

It can happen with a telephone call from an emergency room. Or a divorce summons left in your mailbox. Maybe it happened to you when the doctor said, "Let's talk." Or the baby you just delivered never cried. Perhaps the company downsized; your job was the first to go, then your savings, and now your house. Or, after spending a night in a shelter, you awoke to the unbelievable horror that the hurricane had struck, demolishing everything you owned.

Part of you is numb; the other part, frantic. You detest feeling fragile and you dislike being needy. But you're coming apart at the seams. This is not how you planned your life.

Until now, loss was something that happened to the other person. Perhaps like many of us, you denied its existence by editing it from your life. Unconsciously, you tried to protect yourself by maintaining a comfortable distance from that divorcee next door or that friend battling cancer.

Now you know. This is not how any of us plan our lives. When you least expect it, things happen that can wipe out fields of lavender and years of dreams.[1] Like it or not, loss is an integral part of being a fallen human. Loss is the risk you take for living and loving.

People often say that time heals our grief. Yet time cannot bandage our deepest emotional and spiritual wounds, mend a broken heart, or repair the deep tearing of the soul. Time only provides the room within which you heal. Time is a gift of sacred space. Each day comes packaged with precious pauses and never-to-be-seen-again moments.

Embrace this sacred space even though it feels awfully empty right now. Don't be afraid. You will not stay stuck here. Your God specializes in *what concerns you*. He knows that no two losses are the same. Psalm 34:18 says, ". . . he rescues those who are crushed in spirit." He is the healer. In time, you'll see.

PRAYER PAUSE: *Heavenly Father, I am shaken to the core. I'm not sure that I can face what lies ahead. I don't know what to do next—or even what to say. The only language I have right now is my tears.*

Life is what happens to us while we are making other plans.

THOMAS LA MANCE

2. Okay, I'm in the tunnel; where's the light?

When the darkness
overtakes the godly,
light will come bursting in.

PSALM 112:4

When a ripped tendon needs mending or a broken bone needs fixing, what is one of the first things a member of the healing profession does? Immobilizes it! The doctor restricts its motion *for a limited time* to protect the injury from further trauma. Ripped tendons are wrapped in splints or bandages, skeletal breaks are set in place, then cast in plaster.

When we lose a loved one in death or divorce, our bones don't break, but our heart does. When my twenty-two-year marriage ended in an unwanted divorce, the pain I felt was overwhelming. I wanted to die. Much later I realized that I was experiencing the excruciating ripping apart of what God had joined together. No wonder it hurt so much. I also felt paralyzed between the unknown and the life I knew. Perhaps that is why many wives who have lost husbands speak of feeling immobilized. Cut off from the rest of the world. Enveloped in darkness. It

One Tip for When You're Blue

- *Put on your walking shoes and get some fresh air. Experts claim that a combination of exercise, fresh air, and sunlight are good for what ails you when you feel down.*
- *Map out a short route at first. The next time, increase the distance a block or two.*
- *Be sure to leave your watch at home. Enjoy the simple luxury and glorious freedom of not being on a time schedule.*

feels as if it will always be that way.

You see, near-death survivors aren't the only ones who lay claim to the tunnel experience. One divorced woman says, "It encircled all around my body at arm's length—like a shield." A widow friend of mine describes it this way: "My eyes are wide open, yet I sense I'm in a dark passageway heading toward a pinhole of light."

If that's how you feel, you are not going crazy. And you are not alone. If you sense your life is on hold, you are where you should be. You are in a place of protection, poised for healing.

No one can rush this process. But what we *can* do is trust the Healer. Like a splint or a cast, the state of limbo we are in is *for a limited time*. Psalm 27:1 says, "The Lord is my light and my salvation—so why should I be afraid? The Lord protects me from danger—so why should I tremble?"

But we do tremble. It's normal to be afraid during these dark times when we have tunnel vision. We think every light is an oncoming train. It's because all you and I can focus on is our plight. That's why God wants our eyes on Him. He knows that even the flicker from a single match scatters the darkness when there's no going back and we see no way out. Maybe that's why the psalmist describes God's Word as a light for the path and a lamp for our feet (Psalm 119:105). Our heavenly Father knows every inch of the tunnel and the best route out. While we look for the quickest way, He may want us to wait—until we see Him.

PRAYER PAUSE: *Help me to see, Lord, that you are the only light I need and there are no shortcuts leading to that place of healing.*

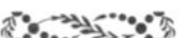

I would rather walk with God in the dark than go alone in the light.

MARY GARDINER BRAINARD

3. Charting my own course through the pain

And the God of all grace, who called
you to his eternal glory in Christ,
after you have suffered a little while,
will himself restore you
and make you strong, firm and steadfast.

1 PETER 5:10 NIV

No one knows better than you do how long you need to grieve. The way you go through your pain is as unique as your loss. Some days you are propelled into situations and toward people that force you to face your loss up close and personal. Each encounter manifests a seamless reminder of unending sorrow. That empty chair at the kitchen table. A letter arriving for the loved one now gone. Your children crying out in the night for their departed daddy. That unavoidable meeting with the lawyer or insurance people to finalize paperwork.

Then there are those moments of floating aimlessly on a sea of denial. Better to avoid the pain than confront it. I remember trying to spare myself the feeling, so I gave in to periodic oblivion, setting myself adrift in a vacuous bubble—unaware of color, the warmth of sunlight, the commute traffic, or the sound of my own voice. The here-and-now lay timeless; the horizon loomed lifeless. At the end of the day, I looked back and realized all I had accomplished was what I knew to do out of routine.

Some moments we are absorbed into the pain. Its rawness obliterates any sense of order. Its desperation comes in towering waves and undulating swells. Forced aground by the randomness of it all, we are plunged beyond tears into silent sobs, amazed that the depth of travail does not consume us.

Wherever grief takes you, you must chart your own course through its staggering unpredictability. There is no time limit. No one way is the right way. No loss is the same. Your loss is uniquely yours, just as my loss is uniquely mine. Some losses are anticipated and lingering; others, unexpected and quick. The greater our loss, the more it meant to us, or the less we were prepared for it, the longer we may need to grieve.

Experts claim that catastrophic loss jolts our entire bodily system. We are forced into emotional overload. As we try to cope with sudden unexpected change, our emotions are drawing eighty-five percent of our energy as mind, body, and spirit fight over the remaining fifteen percent. No wonder we feel physically exhausted, mentally confused, spiritually shaken, and emotionally overwhelmed. It takes time to catch one's balance again.

My friend Shala knows. Shortly before her husband was diagnosed with terminal lung cancer, she was jolted by news that she had Parkinson's disease. "Here I thought Winston would be the one taking care of me," she says. After his death, Shala found comfort among friends also recently widowed. In their company, she wasn't embarrassed to cry. She also attended grief recovery classes and promised herself to take at least a year before she made a move or any major decision.

In contrast, Linda did not have the luxury of time to fully grieve before weighing her options. Within the space of three months, she lost her marriage to divorce and her home in foreclosure and became a single parent. She knows about juggling her own shock and pain along with the emotional and physical needs of her children, who were reeling from their own pain. Some mornings it was all she could do to get out of bed, make their breakfast, and head to work.

As you chart your own unique course, take heart. Remember

that you are doing the best you can with what you know this moment. Applaud yourself for having the emotional wherewithal to do anything at all. Sure, there may be split-second decisions you might later regret, but doesn't everybody eventually regret something? Don't beat yourself up for what you cannot control. For now, what is most important is conserving energy for the journey ahead.

PRAYER PAUSE: *God of all grace, Your word says this suffering I'm going through is just for a little while. I am willing myself to believe that. Stabilize me with Your Spirit because strong, firm, and steadfast are places I haven't reached yet.*

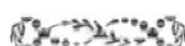

Never be embarrassed by tears.
Loss presses hard
when it writes its signature across our lives.

LAUNA HERRMANN

4. Taking time to honor the loss and myself

You keep track of all my sorrows.
You have collected all my tears in your bottle.
You have recorded each one in your book.

PSALM 56:8

I take comfort in knowing that my Creator is an emotional being who does not treat pain lightly. God knows that sadness is a necessary part of the healing process. He gave us the ability to cry. To Him, each tear is something precious to be treasured and remembered.

Unlike animals, we cry emotional tears that carry to the brain a unique combination of stress-relieving chemicals. Researchers have discovered that we feel better after shedding tears in a stressful situation, whereas suffering in silence can compromise our health. Emotions themselves don't wear us down. What wears us down is expending our life energy on trying to keep our emotions contained.

When you and I weep, we honor our loss by acknowledging the profoundness of what we are going through. After all, Jesus—God the Son—wept (John 11:35). He came to earth to feel what you and I feel and to help us make sense of things. Jesus also wept over Jerusalem (Luke 19:41); and he wasn't embarrassed by crying women. Luke 7:36-50 tells the story of a woman who knelt beside the Savior weeping, her tears falling on his feet. Jesus defended her actions. Since God is not uncomfortable with tears, we shouldn't be either.

In fact, when we express—in words or tears—our feelings about what we have lost, we honor that loss. Our feelings mirror many things: The nature of the loss. Our protest that it happened at all. Our desire to change the outcome—along with the realization that we cannot. Our paralyzing fear that we won't be able to adjust to or even function without what we have lost. When we weep out of anguish or anger, we are reflecting the truth of how the loss is impacting us.

Each time we acknowledge our loss, including the dashed hopes, shattered expectations, and broken dreams, we cooperate with the grieving process that God designed for our healing. Jesus dignifies grief in Matthew 5:4 when He says, "Blessed are those who mourn." Ecclesiastes 3:4 asserts the importance of times to weep and mourn, as well as times to laugh and dance; there is a rhythm to life's seasons.

From my experience with loss, I have learned that while grief is intended only for a season, the memory of a loss lasts a lifetime. Years after a loss, a memory can wash over me and I feel afresh the pain; I honor the loss and myself when I embrace it. You see, the lessons of loss are not about going back, but about looking back, seeing how far we have come, and then moving on. Grief gives us pause to celebrate life as we contemplate both what we have lost and what we have left.

PRAYER PAUSE: *Father, I am so glad You are an emotional being. What a comfort to know the grieving process is not an accident. You created me in Your image to touch the deep hurt in my heart and to grow from it. Help me to remember that You feel what I feel and that not one tear escapes Your notice. I want to honor You by completing this process You have set in motion for my healing.*

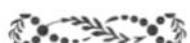

Grief is not an enemy to be conquered.
It is an unwelcomed visitor that will change your life.

DIANE COLE

5. I want to do more than get by

Find rest, O my soul, in God alone;
my hope comes from him.
He alone is my rock and my salvation;
he is my fortress, I will not be shaken.
My salvation and honor depend on God . . .

PSALM 62:5-7 NIV

If this is a preview of the rest of my life, I want no part of it! I remember times of such futility. It seemed like my internal gyro suddenly stopped on tilt. I wasn't making one iota of progress and there appeared no end in sight as I slowly shuffled through my losses. From the inside looking out, I watched the rest of the world laughing and enjoying life, while I could barely function. Listless, I feared that I would remain in suspended animation.

Grief's suspended animation is not how any of us want to live. We hang between facing a reality we cannot change and wanting to believe in the fantasy that nothing *has* changed. The tension is repressive. As a result, we have no sense of accomplishment and little hope that the next day will be any different from the one before.

Some of us were taught that nobody wants to be around weak, needy people who wear emotions on their sleeves. Perhaps that's why we are tempted to avoid the grieving process, because we don't want to be perceived as deficient or vulnerable. We hope that by denying the loss, the pain will go away and we can resume fantasizing that our life will remain as before. In the process, we suppress our own reality. We try to anesthetize ourselves by filling every space on the calendar. We frantically pencil in social activities, lose ourselves working overtime on a job, or keep overly busy with the children.

Suzanna, a teacher in West Virginia, e-mailed me about her determination to make time to grieve the painful loss through divorce of her twenty-eight-year marriage and the ministry she once shared with her evangelist husband. She contrasts her experience with that of a fellow teacher, whose husband died of cancer last year. Suzanna thinks her friend might be making a mistake by avoiding the grieving process with excessive busyness. She does not want to fall into the same trap.

"I could have a pity party the rest of my life, or I could avoid anything that reminds me of the deep pain I'm experiencing," says Suzanna. "Frankly, I am tempted to do both! I compare myself to a video that needs to play at normal speed. I can't put myself on 'pause' or I'll bog down in a grief rut so deep I may never get out. If I try to 'fast forward,' I'll miss what the Lord is trying to teach me."

Wherever you are in this emotional milieu, you are on the right track if you feel suspended, like Suzanna, between dreading the pauses, imagining the fast forwards, and longing for standard play again. Going back to the business of living is fraught with these in-between moments where fantasy seduces and futility reigns. Wanting to postpone the inevitable is normal. Continual denial and avoidance is not.

Feeling the pain is also normal. We only fool ourselves when we keep so busy that we don't have time to feel. Denial is running so fast from ourselves we don't see where we are headed. Eventually grief catches up with us because feeling is the only way to heal the wounds of our heart. In our grief, God wants to teach us how to embrace our sadness, not run from it; how to confront our anger, not stuff it; and how to fully experience each human emotion in between. Our emotions will not stay stuck if we allow grief's divinely ordered stops the necessary time to do their job. Time spent here is not wasted. In fact, experts claim that it is healthier to face your pain when it happens rather than put it off until later.

When you feel, it means you are human and alive, and that there's still hope of better days to come. With each loss I encounter, I rediscover that first I must learn to live these unavoidable moments before I can make it through the day.

PRAYER PAUSE: *Lord, when I feel stuck in suspended animation, help me to not be shaken. May I rest in the security that Your love surrounds me—whatever I am feeling and whenever I chose to grieve. Don't let me anesthetize myself to avoid feeling. Teach me how to be alive again. I want to do more than just get by.*

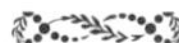

One must never, for whatever reason, turn his back on life

ELEANOR ROOSEVELT

6. Dreaming of chocolate

Taste and see that the Lord is good.
Oh, the joys of those who trust in him!

PSALM 34:8

Chocolate lovers, rejoice! A serving of this delectable confection is good for your heart That's what the American Association for the Advancement of Science recently announced. I don't know about you, but I've been waiting for someone to say those words—especially when I'm feeling down and already have my hand *in* the candy box.

Whenever the pressing *weight* of reality awakens me in the middle of the night, there's nothing quite like dreaming of chocolate, then creeping into the kitchen to see if that half-eaten Hershey® bar is still hidden in the refrigerator egg tray. It's not so much that I need a chocolate *break;* I already know how it feels to be *shattered*. It's just that the smooth creaminess of a chocolate morsel melting in my mouth—before I weaken and chew it—has a way of sweetening my spirit and soothing my heart.

In fact, new research shows that two potential contributors to heart disease—lipid (cholesterol) oxidation and clotted blood vessels—decrease when two or three servings of chocolate are added to our diet. More so, a government survey claims it provides us with essential minerals and healthful antioxidants. Unfortunately, I have a feeling that we won't be hearing the following advice from our doctors any time soon: Rest, drink plenty of fluids, *and take two chocolates*.

Chocolate history is intriguing. Once thought to cure tuberculosis, ulcers, and gout, this potion in its original form of cacao butter was also used to keep weapons from rusting. Conquistadors arriving in "New Spain" discovered that the tiny bean, nicknamed "happie money," was used by the local culture for financial transactions, religious ceremonies, and daily nourishment.[2]

In your personal search for your own "New World," take comfort in the fact that God has His eye on you as you come and go, whether you are waking, sleeping, dreaming—or stumbling upon a box of chocolates. This simplest pleasure can boost your spirit and caress your heart when you need it the most. Maybe that's why researchers are so interested in chocolate. California nutritionist Debra Waterhouse, R.D., author of *Why Women Need Chocolate* (Hyperion, 1994), calls it a good-mood medicine when stress strikes because it elevates serotonin levels in the brain and enhances our well-being.[3]

Come to think about it, chocolate is a metaphor for life's refining process. When roasted and ground, this simple bean from a tropical tree is transformed into chocolate liquor or paste that can be processed into cocoa butter and powder. Cooled, this concoction becomes baking chocolate. One bite of creamy milk chocolate can be beyond your wildest expectations—from its rich velvety appearance to its signature flavor and fragrance as you feel it melting in your mouth. In fact, some of the best chocolate is like life—dark and bittersweet.

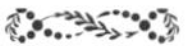

PRAYER PAUSE: *Creator of all things, thanks for simple pleasures. Today's sunrise. Morning coffee. Chocolate.*

Eat chocolate now;
after you're dead there isn't any.

JEAN POWELL

7. God, Tightly hold me in Your arms of mercy

. . . O God, have mercy on me,
for in you my soul takes refuge.
I will take refuge in the shadow of your wings
until the disaster has passed.

PSALM 57:1 NIV

Unrelenting pain has a way of getting our attention and forcing us to our knees—whether thrust upon us by a betrayal, the death of someone close, or other losses. The first thing most of us seek is an end to the suffering or, at least, momentary relief.

What we really need is mercy. Mercy to bear us up when emotions weigh us down. Mercy to keep us from complete destruction (Lamentations 3:22), whether that destruction is self-imposed, accidental, intended by others, or what we deserve. But do you know that no one has a right to mercy?

Mercy is a God-given gift that you and I do not deserve. When I stop to comprehend this fact, I start to appreciate God's goodness in an unpredictable, unsafe world. Yet when my personal circumstances look hopeless and meaningless, I struggle to see God as the giver of anything good. I don't want to hear verses like Psalm 103—how God shows mercy by filling our lives with *good things*. It sounds so phony. That is because pain blinds me to God's goodness.

But, you see, the best of the *good things* is mercy! It reminds us of who we are in Him—daughters of a compassionate King, who is also a forgiving Father. Whether we feel God's presence or not, He has compassion when we suffer (Zechariah 9:12). Because God is the source for all mercy (2 Corinthians 1:3), there is nothing we can do to earn it. The ways God shows mercy during life's emotional moments include:

- When tears are the only language you know, God hears.
- When darkness envelops your way, God sees.
- When pain forces you off course, God stabilizes.
- When loss wears you down, God comforts.
- When grief suspends your progress and saps hope, God remains.

As you read this, you may be wondering, *What kind of a merciful God would allow my husband to abuse me, lie to me, cheat on me, and then abandon me and the children? I lost my job because I had to take time off to be with my sick child; just how did God stabilize me? My husband had a heart attack after the river overflowed its banks last year and we lost our home; I don't feel God's comfort.*

For years, Joni Eareckson Tada struggled with similar issues after a tragic diving accident left her a quadriplegic at age seventeen. She says, "Suffering has a way of taking life out of the abstract, out of the theoretical, making it painfully concrete. Lofty sermons from eloquent Bible teachers don't bring release to people locked in suffering. Ph.D. programs in ivy-walled seminaries don't deliver hope and comfort to those in deep pain." Joni says that when we suffer we must push past theological ideas to a person—"the warm and intimate Person of the Lord Jesus."[4]

This personal side to mercy is evident in the Bible. The Hebrew words for *mercy* in the Old Testament are *rehem*, meaning "softness, mother-compassion" and *hesed*, meaning "loyalty to and belongingness with His own." The New Testament uses two Greek words—*eleos*, meaning "pity and compassion" and *oiktirmos*, meaning "fellow sympathy."[5]

Mercy is a character quality of Almighty God. Merciful is who Jesus is. Because of mercy, we have hope of heaven. We also have hope for the here-and-now, even when we can't feel it, see it, or believe it. Nothing that has happened to us escapes God's notice—certainly not our greatest loss or deepest sorrow. We belong to Him. Sympathetic and compassionate, our Lord wants to enfold us in His arms like a mother gathers a hurting child.

PRAYER PAUSE: *Heavenly Father, Your word says in Hebrews 4:16 to boldly come before you. I don't know why I hesitate. Like a frightened child, I long to snuggle in Your arms of mercy.*

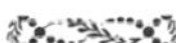

The tears streamed down, and I let them flow as freely as they would, making of them a pillow for my heart. On them it rested.

SAINT AUGUSTINE

About journaling

To process your grief, it is essential to express what your loss means to you. In the telling, you gather together your shattered parts into a whole. What you cannot say aloud to anyone, perhaps you are able to write. Writing helps you recover your ability to speak about unspeakable loss. A journal can become your safe place to let pain and anger emerge.

By acknowledging your deepest thoughts, you affirm what you are going through and develop a more compassionate understanding of yourself. As you sort through your feelings, you release concerns that hold you down and discover insights that grow your spirit, heal your heart, and transform your life. Putting words on paper not only validates your experience in black and white, but provides a record you can look back on someday with surprise and wonder at just how far you have come.

Even jotting down what you are thankful for can develop into a habit. In time, you notice there is usually something positive about each day. In expressing your thoughts and feelings, you are reminded that there are no easy answers or quick solutions. In the process, you gain appreciation for how your life is unfolding. You begin to see flickers of hope along the way, and you are no longer afraid to embrace the moment in front of you.

My Mini Journal of Hope and Gratitude

. . . God, we meditate on your unfailing love. PSALM 48:9

DATE	RIGHT NOW I FEEL	TODAY I AM THANKFUL FOR

If each day is a gift, I'd like to know where to return Mondays.

J. W. WAGNER/
CRABBY ROAD,

Mind-Boggling Moments

That Force Me to Stop and Refocus

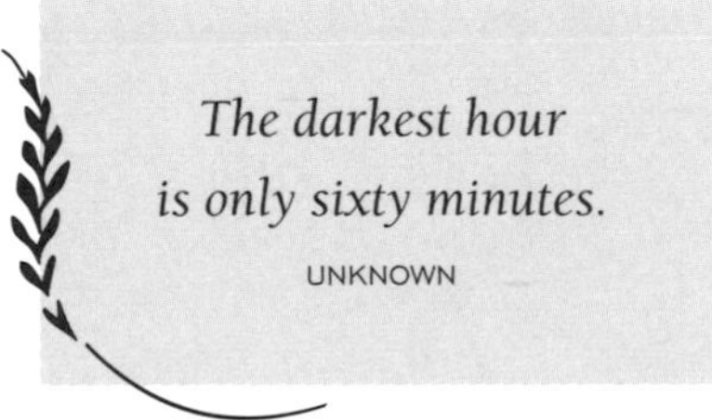

The darkest hour
is only sixty minutes.

UNKNOWN

8. But I can't concentrate

. . . We have no power to face this vast army that is attacking us. We do not know what to do, but our eyes are upon you.

II CHRONICLES 20:12 NIV

Grieving is more than being emotional. It is also a state of being bewildered. A paralyzing mental numbness sets in. The word "discombobulated" fits—there were times my mind limped across fragments of time, then careened into long spaces of apathy before stumbling onto short pauses of clarity.

When our mental clarity erodes, we forget about the bank statements arriving in the mail. The task of reconciling them appears insurmountable. Just thinking about grocery shopping gives way to dread. When the bills need to be paid, we plop them on top of the growing stack on the dining room table. The crush of time does nothing except create more hollowness of thought. Eventually, we don't even notice the paperwork on our desk.

It is difficult to cut through the fog of a divorce without a mental edge. A loss-addled mind can hardly fathom sorting through real estate and personal property appraisals or accountings of liquid and tangible assets. If you are mourning the death of a family member or someone who was close, you wonder if you have the wherewithal to tackle the simultaneous tasks of gathering insurance documents and locating a birth certificate, social security card, or military records. Maybe you are reeling at the thought of a court appearance. Or you are making choices for a funeral or memorial service. So many questions are clamoring for your immediate attention: Do you embalm or cremate? Open casket or closed? Private ceremony or public?

During this mind-boggling time period, one thing most of us wish we could remember is to stop locking our keys in the car! If this has happened to you, you are not alone. Welcome to the ICC Club! (That stands for *I Can't Concentrate.*) The inability to keep your mind on the business at hand is a shared experience. Like King Jehoshaphat, who surveyed the enemy troops gathering in the Tekoa wilderness and saw insurmountable obstacles looming on the horizon, you are not the first to wonder what to do next.

When the familiar props that surround and support us are yanked away, we enter an alien environment. Our daily routine is altered. We are forced into roles we never wanted and for which we may be unprepared. We feel powerless. We have difficulty weighing our options, making decisions, or staying focused when our emotions commandeer our mental energy.

Whatever decisions you face today, do what the king did. Tell God. Keep your eyes on Him as you work with the brain power you have left. Remind yourself that it is okay if rational thought ran away and analytical thinking took a holiday. Tomorrow is another day. You might be surprised. Sometimes a good night's sleep trims obstacles to a more manageable size. Lord willing, by this time next year, your sharp wits and clear thinking will return, along with an eye for details and the memory of an elephant.

PRAYER PAUSE: *Lord, today looms large. I have so much to do at the very time my mental faculties are impaired. I can't articulate—I can't think clearly. Empower me as I try to do what I can.*

Sometimes all we can do when the challenge comes
and we feel our parts flying to their edges is hold on and wait.

GLORIA KARPINSKI

9. I think I am losing my mind

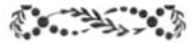

. . . Renew a steadfast spirit within me.

PSALM 51:10 NIV

One of grief's biggest battles is fought in the mind, not at the cemetery or in a divorce court. The weight of our losses can override our mental fortitude to go on. We can't imagine the next day being any different from the one before. Without a mental picture of what the future might look like, we think there is no future. We spiral into the pit of despair described in Psalm 143:7-8. When our thinking is distorted, hopelessness fuels helplessness. Helplessness ignites more hopelessness.

When I spoke recently to a women's group, I shared the story of Gabriele, a baby boy who had suffered from anencephalia, where the flat skull bones and most of the brain are missing. From the third trimester, his parents knew he never had a chance to survive. They chose to carry their son to term so his heart could live on in another child..

His father's response to a reporter's inquiry was this: "We are simple people. When we were told of our baby's condition, we didn't feel up to ending his life. We were ready to face the laws of destiny. . . . We prayed."[6]

Destiny? Standing in those parents' shoes, I'm not sure I would have had enough presence of mind to know what to call it. That mother's pain was excruciating. How do you get through such without losing your sanity? I don't think you do *right away*. You will feel worse before you feel better. You start where you are and do what you can, which some days may be absolutely nothing. There are no clear answers. With that we struggle.

We struggle making sense of a life that ended too soon and the relationship that was taken. We ask why we were chosen to bear the brunt of a random catastrophic loss or an unfaithful mate's recklessness. We question why the good die young and the evil live on and why precious little ones never get a chance. We wonder why our neighbor gets breast cancer and we don't.

I can't help but question why two friends of mine, whose fathers were both pilots in World War II, must live with different outcomes. Why did Regina's dad, whose plane was shot down over Poland, survive a prison camp, while Janey's father was killed? I don't know. There are no answers to life's capriciousness.

What bothers me most is that when life is fickle, it is hard to believe that what happens to us serves a purpose. We are deprived of knowing *what could have been*. The world feels unsafe; our lives, unpredictable. God appears to be on vacation. Without answers, we want to disconnect from the enormity of it all—the startling reality *and* the mystery. Could it be that the loose ends of our lives will never be tied up here on earth, that our inability to comprehend the whole picture is part of an eternal plan? I think so. I think it is where faith begins.

PRAYER PAUSE: *Lord, when I think I'm going crazy, remind me that I'll never figure everything out—I don't have to. What matters is knowing I belong to You. Your Word says, "In him all things hold together" (Col. 1:17). Hold me together, when my emotions and mind are stretched to the breaking point, and there simply are no answers.*

Faith is the art of holding on to things your reason has once accepted, in spite of your changing moods.

C. S. LEWIS

10. Remembering what was

. . . For I have chosen you and I will not throw you away.
Don't be afraid, for I am with you. Do not be dismayed, for I am your God.
I will strengthen you . . . help you . . . uphold you . . .

ISAIAH 41:9-10

Acknowledgment of your loss is critical to healing. It means you are moving forward. To acknowledge that a loved one is gone or a relationship you once enjoyed has ended does not mean that you approve of what happened or agree with it happening at all. By remembering the way things were, you come to terms with how you feel and what you think about it. In the process of integrating your mind with your heart, you become a little more whole.

But there is nothing easy about bearing witness to a wrenching experience. The first time you say "I lost the baby" or "I'm widowed" hurts. I don't know how it feels for a mate or child to die. I do know how it feels to be rejected and betrayed by a spouse I loved and trusted and before whom I bared not only my body, but my mind, heart, and soul. At the time, I could not believe this was happening to me. My divorce was a first in the family.

I vividly recall the first time I said the word aloud. I couched it with "*I think* we're getting a divorce." *Think*? Who was I kidding? In hindsight, I see how embarrassment and shame played a role in my inability to reconcile the reality of how things were with how I wanted them to be.

Many of us struggle with private and public acknowledgment. We try to switch off our thoughts the way we turn off our emotions. We reason that what we do not acknowledge cannot be true. A friend recently told me about a woman who refused to rearrange the furniture in the house after her husband died because she felt disloyal to his memory. It's been fifteen years; she hasn't changed a thing. Perhaps this is the only way she knows to blot out the unthinkable.

With time and your cooperation, it doesn't have to be this way. Perhaps you are beginning to scribble in a journal "the unthinkable" that you cannot admit aloud. Be encouraged to find a way to testify to your loss. If you lost your marriage to a divorce, mull over a treasured memory. Look deep into the faces of a photograph. Realize not all the years were bad. If death claimed your loved one, trace with your fingers the once familiar lines of a signature. Touch an article of clothing. In these simple ways, you are paying tribute to the history you shared with your loved one. You are embracing your loss with a whole heart and a whole mind.

As you bring to mind what your loss means to you personally, remember grief won't last forever. Rejoice. You are in process. Underneath you are God's everlasting arms. Sigh. You are safe. In His holy presence, don't hesitate to weep for yourself. Breathe. You are alive. With each day that follows you will heal a little more. In time, you'll notice that lighter moments are beginning to outnumber the heavy ones.

PRAYER PAUSE: *God, there's something wonderful about knowing that I can't hide from You. You know my unspoken thoughts as clearly as You see into my heart.*

Recognizing what we have done in the past is a recognition of ourselves. By conducting a dialogue with our past, we are searching how to go forward.

KIYOKO TAKEDA

11. *Wishing for what might have been*

O God, have mercy on me. The enemy troops press in on me.
My foes attack me all day long. My slanderers hound me constantly,
and many are boldly attacking me.

PSALM 56:1-2

"Have you ever wondered *what if* you hadn't worked outside the home, maybe your marriage would still be together?" my daughter's sixth-grade Sunday-school teacher asked me. At the time, her words stung. Though I had tried everything to keep my twenty-two year marriage together, I took her remarks personally. I started imagining a different outcome of *if only*. The mind game of *should have, could have*, and *didn't do* had begun.

The instant I closed my eyes that night, the tapes in my brain clicked on. Okay, *what if? What if* I had married somebody else? Perhaps I *should have*. I *could have*. But I *didn't*. Sleep evaded me as I sorted through the archives in my mind, replaying events and conversations. I searched for anything I *could have* overlooked. I even tried rewriting the past into perfect little scenes.

Some of you know what I mean. You are acquainted with this mind game. *What if* you had encouraged your loved one to see a different doctor? Your husband might still be alive. Maybe another physician *could have* found a cure. Perhaps you *should have*. You *could have*. But you *didn't do* it.

What if your family came from a different gene pool? Your daughter would not have been stillborn. Maybe without the complications of cerebral palsy your son would still be alive. Perhaps you *should have* seen a geneticist for testing. You *could have*. But you *didn't* because you believe every life is precious, regardless..

Much of what happens in life is not within our control. We cannot alter our genetic makeup any more than we can rearrange the setting of the sun. We cannot delay the death of those we love any more than we can change the wind's direction. We cannot prevent people from leaving us any more than we can command the rain to go away. Job learned from his experience with catastrophic loss that only our Creator understands why things happen as they do. He alone is in control.

Many of us learn this lesson the hard way. I always do—because I like to be in control. My daughter's former Sunday-school teacher learned the hard way. Ten years after our conversation, her husband divorced her, too. The fact that she had never worked did not change the outcome.

Our lives are peppered with losses, things most of us would never choose. Perhaps the lessons of loss are not about getting life under our control but about giving up control, even when we do not understand the whys and the wherefores.

So if someone should pressure you with, "You *should have, could have, didn't do,*" give a knowing nod. Perhaps your observers have never stood in your shoes. That's okay. Pray they never will. Because unless they experience the disorientation that comes with loss, you cannot expect them to understand how dwelling on *what ifs* wastes time and drains the energy you need in order to go on. You don't have time to linger too long pondering what might have been. You need your wits about you.

PRAYER PAUSE: *God, I'm glad nothing happens to me that is beyond Your understanding, because sometimes I can't figure it out.*

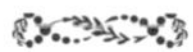

Hindsight is an exact science.

GUY BELLAMY

12. Too much . . . too soon

"I have had enough, Lord," he said. "Take my life. . . ." Then he lay down under the tree and fell asleep.

1 KINGS 19:4-5 NIV

Elijah's words almost mirror my own. "I can't take any more," I wailed at God. In a moment of desperation, I thought about taking my life. I am not alone. If you've thought those thoughts, neither are you. Relentless emotional and mental stress can drive us to the brink of despair.

Do you know that every ninety-four seconds a woman attempts suicide? That is just in the United States. Every eighty-six minutes a woman commits suicide. The silent scream for help ricochets across the heavens more times than we think.

"I was sucked down into a whirlpool of depression, and I was fighting for my life," says Jane from South Dakota. For years, Jane bore more than her share of burdens. She had survived not only her husband's announcement on their twenty-fifth anniversary that he didn't love her anymore, but his earlier admission of cheating when their son was two years old. Next came the discovery of her husband's involvement in pornography, the eventual divorce, and his phone call announcing his marriage to a long-time coworker.

"I felt I was being pushed over the edge," she says. "I wasn't prepared for the feelings of failure as a woman and a wife." Jane talks about how she went as far as making an audio tape outlining her requests before driving 400 miles to ask her sister about raising her two children in the event she "couldn't take it anymore."

Whenever the load we carry seems more than we can bear, we

may consider ending our life because we cannot fathom enduring more of the same. Perhaps you have felt this heaviness as caretaker for a family member with Alzheimer's disease or cancer. If so, you know how vulnerable you can be.

As your loved one's health deteriorated, you watched her face other losses—the loss of mental faculties and physical abilities, activities, independence, pride, and self-image. She was never quite the same. You aren't either. You were forced to learn a new way to genuinely relate to and to radically love a different person. You told yourself: No pity. No patronizing. No false guilt, even over all the times you muttered under your breath. Eventually, both of you lost the full enjoyment of each other's company.

In the end, you may reason that death relieved your loved one's suffering and you never gave a second thought to your own spent emotions. Besides, there was no time or energy to focus on your needs. Others might call you selfish if you had.

Maybe you never realized until now that you have been grieving a long time. For months or maybe years, you silently mourned this lingering illness that came between you and the one you loved. For the first time, you are seeing that each of you longed in your own way for life to be as it was before. Now in the face of so much change, you are fighting for the will to go on.

"Thinking about suicide is the devil's work," says Jane. "He wants you to dwell on your broken dreams, to keep looking backwards, and to believe your situation is hopeless." She advises: Share your feelings with a friend. Get into a support group or counseling. Ask your doctor for an antidepressant. Read books dealing with your problem. Be faithful with your devotions. Pray.

What helped me battle darkness, after I discovered my husband's long-term affairs, are the words of Isaiah 26:3—"Thou wilt keep him in perfect peace, whose mind is stayed on thee" (KJV). Whenever I imagined him with other women, I repeated this verse I had memorized as a child. With repetition and time that "sword of the spirit" shut off the mental horror.

As you read the Bible, when a verse gives you encouragement or inspiration, write it out and even memorize it. If you are ever pushed to the edge and feel under attack, your spiritual arsenal will be stocked with a variety of "Old" and "New" swords to choose from. According to Ephesians 6:10-18, during the battle for your mind, they can help you *stand firm* against the unseen powers of darkness, the deceptive strategies and manipulative tricks of the devil. And after the battle, you will *still be standing firm*.

PRAYER PAUSE: *Father God, keep me on my feet as I battle death and darkness in my struggle for light and life.*

You don't get to choose how you're going to die. Or when. You can only decide how you're going to live. Now.

JOAN BAEZ

13. That one thing I must do today

My times are in your hands. . . .

PSALM 31:15 NIV

- *There are so many items on my to-do list, where do I start?*
- *Whose needs do I take care of first when I have so many of my own?*
- *How do I manage my work day when I can't remember to put out my trash?*

Sound familiar? You bet. Coping with loss can easily stress our already chaotic lives to the point of overload. Experts claim the death of a family member or a divorce causes profound stress. Often the mind's only course of action is to shut down. Anxiety, depression, or a nervous breakdown can occur—unless we take action. But who needs one more thing to do?

Dr. Richard Swensen, author, physician, and associate professor of medicine at the University of Wisconsin Medical School, believes we need margin to prevent overloaded lives. He defines margin as the opposite of overload; it is the difference between our load and our limit.

"What would you think if this page had no margins? What would be your opinion of the publishers if they tried to cram the print top to bottom and side to side so that every blank space was filled?" Swensen writes. "The result would be aesthetically displeasing, hard to comprehend, and probably even chaotic. Like some of our lives."[7]

Only you know the load you can handle. Unless you maintained a reserve space for adjusting to and surviving unexpected life events, grief can push you past your limit. You cannot change what has happened, but you can begin right now to create this necessary space. Start by pausing to rethink your priorities and regroup. Whenever you glance at your frantic schedule and give yourself permission to say, "No, I can't take this on right now," you leave room for what you *can* do. You are on your way to restoring the emotional and mental energy that grieving depletes.

By putting margin back in life, you gift yourself with grace. You quit judging your performance by the items completed on that to-do list. You stop blaming yourself when you don't have it together. You pare down your priorities to the size you can handle. Your speech slows. The nervous twitches cease. Within this space you rediscover you still have choices. You begin to live a more serene, deliberate life.

As a single parent, I lived a frantic life with little or no margin. Each morning my alarm sounded at six o'clock. I dressed, made breakfast, then packed lunches for my daughter and myself. I commuted two hours on the freeway to work a full-time job to put a roof over our heads, clothes on our backs, and food on the table. Also, I was a mother, bill-payer, home maintenance worker, cook, house cleaner, homework tutor, and taxi driver, to name a few positions. Evenings and weekends I juggled these "at home" jobs with office paperwork that needed to be researched, printed, and proofread. Most nights and many weekends, I plopped into bed long after midnight.

My heart pounded and my mind raced from the overload. Unable to focus on what to do first or next, I paced the house, overwhelmed with all I had to do. One particular weekend I remember telephoning my father, who lived back east. My thoughts rambled. My words were rapid, short, choppy. Dad listened, then said, "Make a list of what needs to be done. Next, prioritize it by numbers. Today, concentrate only on what is number one on that list. Tomorrow is another day."

That simple advice can save your sanity. You might wonder why you didn't think of it—if you weren't so overwhelmed. I know the feeling. I also know that although margin won't pay your bills or complete your to-do list, it will enlarge your capacity to cope.

PRAYER PAUSE: *Lord, I tremble just thinking about all the things I must do today. Show me what I need to accomplish today. Then, help me leave the rest in Your hands.*

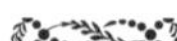

I love a broad margin to my life.
Sometimes, in a summer morning, having taken my accustomed bath,
I sat in my sunny doorway from sunrise till noon, rapt in a revery.

HENRY DAVID THOREAU

14. Sovereign Lord, please order my day.

The Lord will work out his plans for my life. . . .

PSALM 138:8

I stood in the parking lot fumbling for my car keys. For the second day in a row my job had canceled. *I can't believe this! I drove all this way to learn the meeting was rescheduled? Does anybody realize what this means?* I forced back tears, knowing too well the impact. Another day without pay. No compensation for my daughter's daycare expense, for my travel time, or the gasoline consumed during the 100-mile round-trip drive. I was nearing the edge of panic.

Then I recalled the words of a friend, who also worked as an independent contractor: "When I get in a 'tiz and start to worry about making ends meet, I *stop* and I pray, 'Lord, order my day!'"

Regina's words were credible because she knew the territory. She, too, was a single mom fighting to survive financially. Her advice helped me come to terms with the forced stops in my own life that I could neither anticipate nor control.

On the drive home that morning, I remembered that I had already asked God to order my day. That meant things were happening the way they should. Instead of panicking, I decided to use the quiet time in the car to rethink the rest of the day. *Okay, I didn't make any money; but I do have proofreading to finish. The rug needs vacuuming. I could clean a closet. Maybe I'll surprise Melanie with homemade cookies.* By the time I pulled into my driveway, I had refocused on the positive things I could do and off the negatives that feed my fears and fuel self-pity. For the remaining hours, I lived believing that whatever happened, God was in charge.

Nobody ever said this kind of living is easy. You must begin anew each day. Some days I forget. Other days, I can't pull it off. Living beneath the bleak cover of impending doom, whether real or imagined, can leave the best minds in a whirl. It's mind-boggling going through the grieving process with its ensuing changes, whether they are financial or relational. To survive you need a Master planner.

When you pray for God to order your day, you set aside your personal plans. It's like you hand Him the menu and say, "You choose for me." You are asking for His will to be accomplished in your life—whenever and however He wants to do it. As you open yourself up to accept that things will happen the way they should, you free God to work in your heart and mind.

One day at a time, you lean a little further into His sovereignty. You start trusting Him for both the *right-nows* of life and the far-off future. Along the way, you discover you are spending more moments with Him and more time praying, "Lord, order my day—then, help me accept whatever you send." You begin to believe that nothing escapes His attention or happens to you that He does not sanction first (Proverbs 16:9). There isn't a more radical way to live than when you dare to say, "If the Lord wills. . . ."[8]

PRAYER PAUSE: *Almighty God, teach me to pray as Jesus prayed that night on the Mount of Olives, "I want your will, not mine."*[9]

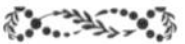

What God expects us to attempt,
He also enables us to achieve.

STEPHEN OLFORD

My Mini Journal of Hope and Gratitude

O, Lord, . . . You know my every thought . . . PSALM 139:1,2 NLT

DATE	MY MIND BATTLES ARE	TODAY I WILL FOCUS ON

Courage is not the absence of fear; it's the mastery of it. BENJAMIN FRANKLIN

No man can think clearly when his fists are clenched.
GEORGE JEAN NATHAN

Nurturing Moments

For Accepting My Body's Limitations

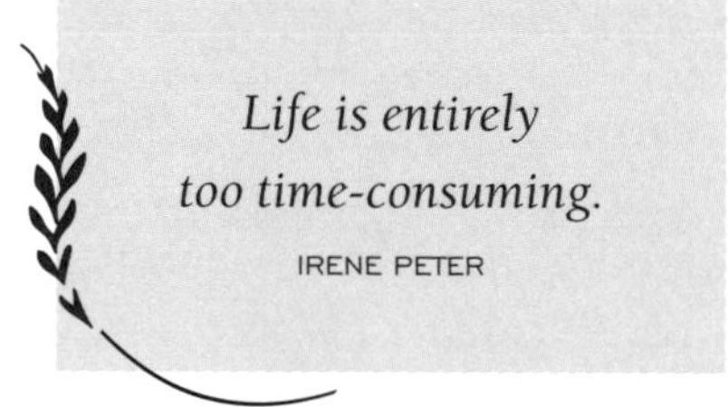

Life is entirely too time-consuming.

IRENE PETER

15. Giving myself permission to . . .

Death had its hands around my throat; the terrors of the grave overtook me. I saw only trouble and sorrow. Then I called on the name of the Lord. . . . and then he saved me. Now I can rest again, for the Lord has been so good to me. He has saved me from death, my eyes from tears, my feet from stumbling.

PSALM 116:3-8

Loss jolts our foundation, moving us off center. First, we are unsure of our footing, emotionally and mentally. Then, cracks develop in our physical health. If the loss is unexpected, the shock creates sudden stress.

Stress sets off an avalanche of chemicals in our body. The brain tells nerves to send adrenaline to the muscles and signals the pituitary gland to release corticotrophin into the bloodstream. Soon the body is inundated with stress hormones from noradrenaline to cortisol and glucocorticoids. Sugar is released as quick energy for the fight or flight ahead.

While you are deciding what to do, your body is gearing up. The heart pumps faster. Blood pressure rises. Perspiration increases. Breathing accelerates. Digestion slows. Memory quickens. Eventually, the production of stress hormones will cease—a necessary design so your body won't burn itself out. However, one tense situation after another can keep these hormones elevated and leave you vulnerable to health problems, memory loss, and fatigue. Unrelenting stress can feel like a death grip.

You may be acquainted with this death grip. You understand why the psalmist speaks of his throat being constricted. You may complain more often of backaches or headaches. Allergies flare.

You have little energy. The normal distress experienced during the grieving process may not directly make you ill, but can indirectly affect your appetite and sleep patterns.

If there was ever a time to give yourself permission to take care of your body, this is it. Applaud it for getting you this far. Nourish it with a balanced diet. Replenish its fluid levels daily with at least eight glasses of water. Walk it around the block. Relax it with a cat nap. Monitor its intake of stimulants, such as excess caffeine. Take it to the doctor to ease any concerns you have.

During this time of distress, reassure yourself that you are in good hands. As you struggle to put one foot in front of the other, pray for your health. God will not forget you. Your name is written on the palm of His hand (Isaiah 49:16).

PRAYER PAUSE: *Creator God, I continue to be amazed how You designed me to function in a crisis situation. I know that stress is an inescapable part of life, especially during times of profound loss. As I begin my day, I ask You to protect this marvelous body You have given me. I place my very life into Your hands.*

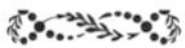

One never notices what has been done,
one can only see what remains to be done!

MARIE CURIE

16. *Leaving the dusting 'til dawn*

My heart is like wax, melting within me.
My strength has dried up like sunbaked clay.

PSALM 22:14B, 15A

If there's one thing you don't have to worry about right now, it is too much "Martha Stewart." When you can barely drag your own body through the day, you won't be inviting the neighbors in for a feast, carving a six-foot ice sculpture centerpiece with your chain saw, or single-handedly baking and filling 500 cream puffs for dessert.

Do not be discouraged if you can't manage ten things to do and three people to cook for with zero energy. Weariness is a normal dimension of grief.

So is lack of sleep. Gone *(forever, it seems)* are nights when sleep comes quickly and easily and dreams are serene. Rest, if any, is fitful at best. If you are tossing and turning, you are not peculiar—or alone.

Sleep research reveals that sixty-five percent of Americans are sleep deprived. Without sufficient sleep, any one of us will experience fatigue and become discouraged. Lack of sleep also affects cognitive and motor skills such as concentration and driving. The stress hormone cortisol elevates in the bloodstream. Insufficient sleep also alters dream patterns.

"Dreaming is a mood-regulatory process that helps you get rid of anger and other emotional issues," says Rosalind Cartwright, Ph.D., director of a sleep disorder center in Chicago. Cartwright says that you are more likely to awaken after a negative dream "which puts you in a bad mood and colors your whole day."[10]

Regaining physical stamina after a major loss does not happen overnight. It is as much a process as recovering emotional and mental well being. Many days you feel worn out. All you want to do is plop in a chair or take a nap.

Looking back, I realize that those Saturday afternoons when I curled up on the couch with my cat for a half hour were not wasted moments. Sleep is the best thing we can do for our bodies when we are bone weary from the hard work of grieving.

Grief won't wait, but the dusting can. You guard your physical health when you make rest a priority. If you are a housecleaning freak like I *was*, take comfort in a recent opinion poll funded by Kimberly-Clark that shows twenty percent of us say our standards have declined over the years. Reasons cited include:

- Lack of time
- More to life than cleaning
- Too many other demands
- Isn't important enough
- Will just get dirty again

The next time guilt envelops you, throw it off. Get cozy under a quilt instead. Tell the clutter around you and the dust on the counter, "Hush!" Remember that Martha Stewart rarely does on-site inspections . . . unless you're a regular subscriber. Then, you are on your own—because she's got your address.

PRAYER PAUSE: *Lord, after the heat of this morning's adrenaline rush, my energy has evaporated. I finally understand why David uses words like "melting within me" and "dried up." Refresh my ravaged body with the restoring power of sleep.*

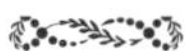

It was such a lovely day I thought it was a pity to get up.

W. SOMERSET MAUGHAM

17. Getting the upper hand on stress

But let all who take refuge in you be glad; let them ever sing for joy. Spread your protection over them, that those who love your name may rejoice in you. For surely, O Lord, you bless the righteous; you surround them with favor as with a shield.

PSALM 5:11, 12 NIV

Stress can work for you. Your body may be telling you not to push beyond your capacity. But most of us don't pay attention. Instead of taking care of ourselves, we work harder, either out of necessity or to distract ourselves from grief. Tension builds in our neck and shoulders—we clench our jaw, grind our teeth, and tighten our grip. We dismiss the healing touch of a hand.

"Please take care of *yourself*," I recall my mother saying. "Find time each day to make yourself go limp in a chair." At the time, I heard her words, but I did not heed the advice. I was too busy. Mother had flown out to help during the hectic two-week period I downsized from the family home to a single-parent household. On weekends, we sorted through the accumulation of two decades of marriage. While I was at work, she boxed pots and pans. At night, we both packed. After the move, we unpacked.

Long after my mother's visit, I maintained this hectic pace. My stomach was in knots. I lost weight. My heart raced. I caught one cold after another. Whipped to a frenzy, I had lost the appreciation for what maintains and sustains life—breathing, walking, sleeping, touching. I needed to reconnect.

When my friend Sharon suggested a facial, I resisted. *I don't have time for such nonsense!* Looking back, I now wonder why I waited so long. Once the esthetician swathed my face in cleansing lotion, I knew how much I missed being touched. When she remarked about my clenched jaw and furrowed brow, I had to admit Mother was right—it was time to go limp in my chair.

Loss has a way of forcing us into the unfamiliar. Before my divorce, I never thought to take care of myself. I never pondered the importance of touch. Until there is no longer a hand entwined in yours, no affirming pat on the back, no shoulder to cry on, you do not know how separated you can feel. Sadly, it's often when you need a hug the most that people around you will feel the most awkward. They can't figure out when or if it is okay to hug you.

Touch represents our connection with the rest of humanity. It is the first sense infants develop and the last sense to fade as we age. Experts say touch heals by lifting depression, boosting our immunity, and relieving stress. They claim a massage reduces anxiety and sadness, lowers levels of the stress hormone cortisol, and alters our brain waves so we feel more relaxed and alert.

When stressed, we cannot afford to wait for others to initiate contact. We must learn to reach out and make touch happen. You can begin by looking for a simple touch in an ordinary way. Start with your hair dresser. Treat yourself to a manicure. Try a pedicure. Think about that facial. Consider a neck and shoulder massage. And if asking for a hug feels uncomfortable, then perhaps it is time to discover the healing touch you are missing. Maybe it's time to go limp in a chair and take care of you.

PRAYER PAUSE: *Lord, I long for Your merciful touch. Spread Your protection over me. Being uptight all the time is not living.*

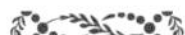

Devils can be driven out of the heart
by the touch of a hand on a hand.

TENNESSEE WILLIAMS

18. Creating minute vacations just for me

How precious are your thoughts about me, O God. They are innumerable!
I can't even count them; they outnumber the grains of sand!
And when I wake up in the morning, you are still with me!

PSALM 139:17, 18

Are you longing for a respite from your sorrow? You know you need one after all you have been through. Getting away from the day-in-and-day-out living with loss is as necessary as taking time off from a regular routine. Vacation time is never wasted time. It can regenerate the heart, quiet the mind, relax the body, and nourish the soul. Our Creator never intended us to live in a continual state of anguish and tension—or sorrow.

Jesus modeled time away. After learning of John the Baptist's death, ". . . he went off by himself in a boat to a remote area to be alone" (Matthew 14:13). After bringing Lazarus back to life (John 11:54), feeding the five thousand (Matthew 14:23), and healing a man with leprosy (Luke 5:13-16), our Savior sought out a time of solitude. The bookends of his ministry are about time away—beginning with the forty days he spent alone in the wilderness (Matthew 4:2) and ending with the hours spent in Gethsemane. Jesus knew the exhaustion of grief. Mark 14:34 describes his soul as "crushed with grief to the point of death."

Grieving is hard work. As we labor giving birth to life after loss, we need time away. Time to contemplate what is behind and what is ahead. Time to pray for God's will. Time away to replenish the blood we lose and the energy we expend coming to terms with the reality that death is final, loss remains, and life goes on.

Start where you are. Make time away your friend. All you need is a minute. Tonight, bathe your restless thoughts in warm remembrances of God's help in the past. Tomorrow, savor His creation in front of you—a flower's fragrance, shells on a beach, the rustle of tree leaves, dogs bolting after cats, a lake lapping the shore. If you don't have access to a wilderness of your own, make one. Turn your car into a sanctuary during the commute to work by shutting off the radio. Stroll around the block on your lunch hour. Roll out a blanket beneath a shady park tree and plop down a while. Enjoy a longer shower.

You can also create a minute vacation by reliving a time that was good. Pull out memories of walking barefoot in summer or tossing snowballs in winter. Remember how it feels to soak up sunlight or tilt your face toward the rain. Once again imagine the sights, smells, and sounds of spring. Deep sorrow sharpens our awareness of and appreciation for life. When we take these "I am present in the moment" trips, we begin to see the world in a brighter light.

PRAYER PAUSE: *Creator God, how I long for a day off from the strain of deep sorrow. Enable me to see from Your viewpoint that a day off and an off day each have value and are clocked the same. Show me the value of momentary time away. I want to dig my toes into the warmth of Your endless thoughts toward me. Your Word says they are more numerous than grains of sands along the seashore.*[11]

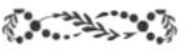

Solitude is not something you must hope for in the future.
Rather, it is a deepening of the present.

THOMAS MERTON

19. Finding the slow, still person inside

Be still, and know that I am God.

PSALM 46:10 NIV

When is the last time you sat in stillness? No telephone. No noise from the television. No demands from the children. Seems impossible, doesn't it? Often life is too noisy and we are too busy for quiet reflection. With so much mind chatter and body movement, we have forgotten where we left the slow still person inside us. Many of us don't know how to find our way back.

We lose our way even more so when we grieve. We are afraid to be still. We fear being caught alone with our sorrow. Our responses to those around us become distorted. Others sense that we are out of sync. We alternate between filling every day on our calendar with mundane activities to canceling important appointments. Either we talk incessantly on the telephone or we take it off the hook. Our concept of time dulls or intensifies much like our temperament swings from resignation to rage. "I'm not myself," we say. We may panic, desperate to recover our shattered self.

When we are frantic to be at peace, stillness is what we need the most; but it's what we want the least. As nature abhors a vacuum, we dread a quiet moment because disquieting memories rush to fill it. Perhaps that's why we don't see stillness as the starting point for soothing our emotions and settling our mind. Instead, we think of it as an end in itself—a quick fix to our frenzy. But stillness is so much more. It provides the environment to slow us down and to bring us home again to inner peace. Stillness gives us opportunity to become acquainted with and glean wisdom from our life experiences without agenda.

But how do we reign in our restlessness and fears so we can be still? Where do we look for our slow person within? What happens when we know circumstances won't be changing any time soon and we are certain we will never again feel at peace?

Mind-over-matter gurus tell us to "Think peace" while motivational speakers advise "Think positive," as if a positive, peaceful thought would change reality. What *do you do next* after you think peace, even pray for peace; but there is no peace? Maybe that's the point. Peace is not a mind-set or a truce with life. It is not a result of something you and I do. Peace doesn't suddenly appear *if* we possess all the right things, *when* we are with the right person, or *because* we pray for God to do things our way. God never promised to change our circumstances, end our conflict, or stop our pain. But He does promise to go with us *through* it. The paradox is that while we want to see our life back in order, our Creator wants to show us Himself.

Stillness is not an enemy we must fear. Stillness beckons us to go deeper. The moment we stop struggling and start believing that God ". . . will make it happen," we find He is waiting for us right where He has always been (Psalm 46:10).[12] God is the source of peace. His presence is our peace.

PRAYER PAUSE: *Lord, I am glad You are not stopped by what unnerves, confuses, or perplexes me. Help me submit to the grieving process as You slow me down so You can show me yourself.*

I do not want the peace which passeth understanding,
I want the understanding which bringeth peace.

HELEN KELLER

20. Getting over the guilt about relaxing

My soul finds rest in God alone. . . .

PSALM 62:1 NIV

I finally met lollygagging and dillydallying—and I like them! However, it has taken years to get acquainted. I am one of those people who was brought up believing that "idle hands are the devil's workshop." I never stopped to question what *I needed*—until the loss of my marriage. I just kept moving and doing.

The other day I was on the telephone with my friend, Regina. We were complaining about the stress in our lives. She reminded me of what I once told her—"Someday I want *to be caught* sitting in my living room chair reading." You see, the two of us have a lot in common. We feel guilty if, when, and after we spend time relaxing. We were taught to carry the Proverbs 31 woman to an extreme.

This is especially true if you were used to caring for another who is no longer in your life. The space they once filled feels empty. Your heart says you must rush to fill that gaping hole with productive activity or with another relationship. You are afraid that if you don't, you will be sucked into its oblivion. The body has a way of sensing this tension in the heart. Your body may be telling you that now is not the time to rush but to relax.

Relaxation helps us regain perspective and stay centered. We start noticing simple things all around us that can nurture us back to life. We begin to linger longer than usual over the morning cup of coffee. We take a moment to shrug our shoulders and sigh to release tension. We notice our clenched fist and slowly uncurl our fingers to run them through our pet's fur. Before we know it, that cat is occupying our lap or we're taking the dog for a walk.

Well, lollygagging and dillydallying are waiting to meet you. They can add years to your life and sparkle to your eyes. You can start relaxing now. Stop apologizing for pausing to window shop while you run errands. No more excuses for not taking a moment by your desk to stretch your neck muscles, flop your feet, or apply Chapstick®. And if somebody catches you sitting in your living room chair reading, don't leap into action. Isn't it time to get over the guilt about relaxing?

PRAYER PAUSE: *Father, help me relax in the very center of this empty space that surrounds me. I don't want to feel guilty any more for what I can't change, control, did, or didn't do. Beginning right now, I want to enjoy this day, as I rest secure in Your love for me.*

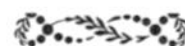

This instant is the only time there is.

GERALD JAMPOLSKY

21. *Jesus, please take this load off my feet!*

I cry out to God Most High, to God who will fulfill his purpose for me.

PSALM 57:2

Grieving is not an event that happens to you but an action you undertake to process loss. You *carry* the load. You *bear* the burden. You *brace* yourself beneath the weight—an emotionally, mentally, and physically oppressive weight your humanity was never created to bear alone.

Jesus spoke about such weight in Matthew 11:28-30. In talking about the weariness of heavy burdens, He also mentions taking on His yoke. Metaphorically, *yoke* implies subjection. It is a teaming up with another, as oxen linked to plow a field or horses harnessed together to pull a wagon. Throughout the Bible, several Greek and Hebrew words for *yoke* are translated *burden,* implying a load to be lifted and carried, such as by a pack animal.

Using that combined imagery we can visualize how God wants to undergird us with His presence when we grieve. Shoring up the load. Redistributing the weight. Sharing the burden. When we submit to being yoked with God, we do not struggle alone. Together, we undertake the process of working through our losses. The weight of our sorrow is transferred to Him.

Only you know the load you carry—because only you know how much you have lost. A companion. A child. Family. Friends. Your health. Hope for the future. A dream. Purpose. Your ability to trust. Perhaps your identity in the community as somebody's wife. The place you once called home. Maybe your faith.

Whatever your losses and wherever you are in the grieving process, God is seeking access to your pain. Your concerns are His concerns. He longs to come beside you, to join with you, and to bear you up.

In 1875, Hannah Whitall Smith, wife of an internationally acclaimed evangelist and mother of four, wrote *The Christian's Secret to a Happy Life*. She tells the tale of a wagon driver offering a ride to a man bent over with a heavy burden. The man accepted the ride but kept the load on his shoulders. When the driver asked why he didn't lay it down, the man explained that it was enough for the driver to carry him; that he couldn't expect his burden to be carried, too. Too often we are like that man. We keep life's weight strapped to our back.

Throughout her life, Hannah bravely bore more than her share of burdens—her personal battle with arthritis, a philandering husband along with the resultant public scandal and loss of friends, the death of her son to scarlet fever, one daughter abandoning her husband for an artist, and another daughter abandoning her faith to marry atheist Bertrand Russell. But unlike the man in her story, Hannah knew life's load was too oppressive to carry alone. She surrendered her self-sufficiency and discovered God's outstretched arms waiting to undergird her.

PRAYER PAUSE: *Lord, teach me to be willing to come under Your yoke. As I mentally plop my worn-to-a-frazzle body into Your strong arms, I release what concerns me right now.*

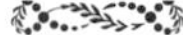

There is nothing the body suffers the soul may not profit by.

GEORGE MEREDITH

My Mini Journal of Hope and Gratitude

He renews my strength . . . PSALM 23:3 NLT

DATE	MY STRESSES RIGHT NOW	TODAY I WILL SLOW DOWN BY

I hate housework! You make the beds, you do the dishes—and six months later you have to start all over again. JOAN RIVERS

Don't ask me to relax. It's my tension that's holding me together.
UNKNOWN

SMILE AS YOU PLACE THIS SIGN ON YOUR REFRIGERATOR.

This is a self-cleaning kitchen
You eat. You clean

Soul-Searching Moments

When I Am Honest With God

Relying on God has to begin all over again every day as if nothing yet had been done.

C. S. LEWIS

22. *Is God on vacation, or what?*

My soul is downcast within me . . .
I say to God my Rock, "Why have you forgotten me?
Why must I go about mourning?"

PSALM 42:6, 9 NIV

"Life in the Lord is combat," says Jon Drury, a pastor in Castro Valley, California. This is especially true when we are ambushed by loss. As loss puts faith to the test and our minds put God on the spot, the battle intensifies. Major skirmishes are fought on the spiritual front of grief.

Bewildered by the silence of a God who seems not to hear our prayers, we wonder how to pray. Maybe we are unable to focus on Scripture at the very time we are besieged with an onslaught of questions. Our tender hearts can be easily impaled by others' glib responses—"Be glad it's over. It was for the best. If you had only had more faith. You need to pray more."

If you feel under attack and are spiritually shaken, it does not mean that something is wrong with you or your faith—or that God is absent or uncaring. Loss hurts, whether you believe in God or not. Faith has never been an insurance policy against loss, and it never will be. It is not a hedge around heartbreak, a quick fix for pain, or a detour through grief. While faith can act like a shock absorber during grief and provide you with an eternal perspective as you struggle to make sense of your life, it does not offer immunity from sorrow or absolution from questioning what you believe.

Divorce put my faith to the test. I could not understand why the God who hates divorce had not restored my marriage. With hindsight, I now see my unanswered prayers were part of a larger plan. God was drawing me to Himself and positioning me to handle the impact of my former husband's infidelity before that truth came to light. But during those dark, disappointing days, as I grieved the loss of my marriage and struggled to believe God still had plans for my life, there were occasions I thought God was vacationing in the Holy Land.

Be encouraged in your time of grief that it is common to struggle to believe. It is not necessarily that your faith is too little or too weak. Like the little boy who stood in a room full of manure and knew there was a pony in there somewhere, you stand in faith each time you dare to hope and trust in what you cannot see.[13] Your unanswered prayers do not mean God is deaf to your cries. Because you can't sense His presence or understand what He is up to does not mean He has forgotten or abandoned you. As you will soon see, our God is a God who keeps His promises.

PRAYER PAUSE: *God, my faith is shaken. How do I continue to believe in a loving, caring heavenly Father when You allow your children to suffer unspeakable loss, shattering disappointment, and excruciating pain? All I want is my life back in order. Is that too much to ask? Sometimes I think You are mad at me, because You feel so far away. Yet I sense behind Your seeming absence and veil of silence that You are nearer than I realize. Guide me with Your grace as I struggle to believe.*

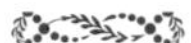

Faith is knowing there's an ocean
because you've seen a brook.

AUTHOR UNKNOWN

23. Lately, I don't want to read my Bible

I lie in the dust, completely discouraged; revive me by your word. . . .
I weep with grief; encourage me by your word.
Keep me from lying to myself; give me the privilege of knowing your law.

PSALM 119:25, 28-29

When you are hurting, one spiritual discipline that gets pushed aside is Bible reading. Take it from one who knows, study guides can be intimidating when you have little energy and no enthusiasm to look up the required verses. So what do you do? You don't want to leave life-giving insights etched only on the pages of your Bible but to experience them in a practical way. You long for a faith that makes sense today—not someday after you reflect upon it. You yearn for a *right-now* certainty that the God in whom you place your confidence understands what you are going through *this moment* and that He has something to tell you *now*.

I remember picking up my Bible and feeling so rattled I didn't know where to start. How I longed for peace of mind to get to sleep and a reason to get up the next day. In desperation—perhaps a little like that pushy woman who pressed through the crowd to touch Christ's garment, believing she would get well—I decided to hold God to His promises. I figured I had little left to lose. At the time, I didn't realize the extent to which the Lord would use His Word to revive my heart and revamp my life.

I began by writing "List of Promises" at the top of a legal pad. In the left margin, I jotted down the current date. Then, I opened my Bible in what I call the Russian roulette style; meaning, on any page that opened, I looked for a verse. Next, I listed the phrases that caught my eye and underlined a promise I could apply to my life. Finally, I prayed for courage to believe it.

On those occasions when apathy and discouragement had me in their vice grip, I reread the promises I had previously listed. What an eye opener! I was astonished by God's faithfulness not only during the last few days but the past weeks and months. That tear-stained legal pad provided the proof I needed to keep willing myself to believe *one more day* that I could and would survive. It also documented my spiritual journey as well, and eventually evolved into a journal from which I wrote *When He Leaves* years later. The following is a sample entry:

Tues., January 12 —Acts 20:32 God and his word—the word of his grace—can build me up.
—II Peter 1:3-11 His divine power has given us all we need for life and godliness.

I realize this is not a recommended in-depth method for studying the Bible. This is merely a technique for getting back into the Scriptures when you are searching for a promise to hold on to or struggling to see what God is teaching you. In your hurt and confusion, God will meet you where you are.

PRAYER PAUSE: *Lord, show me a promise I can cling to in these moments I've set aside to spend with You alone.*

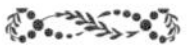

Every happening, great and small,
is a parable whereby God speaks to us,
and the act of life is to get the message.

MALCOLM MUGGERIDGE

24. Asking "Why Me? How come now?"

People can never predict when hard times might come. Like fish in a net or birds in a snare, people are often caught by sudden tragedy.

ECCLESIASTES 9:12

Loss always provokes us to ask, "Why?" Why did my father leave me? Why was my husband killed? Why did I miscarry? Why did he rape me? Why must I agree to a divorce? Why am I in this wheelchair? Why me? . . . And how come now?

We have been asking "Why?" since Adam and Eve ate the forbidden fruit that ushered us into a fallen world of good *and evil*, where bread molds, weeds invade our gardens, and people get sick, grow old, and die. Scripture is replete with our resultant disappointments: Job arguing with God; David asking why; the disciples prodding for why a man was born blind; Mary and Martha wondering why Jesus allowed their brother to die. Even Jesus inquired why God had abandoned him.[14]

Trish Schuster knows that those left behind by suicide victims are always asking why. Five years ago, her daughter, Dawn, shot herself. Dawn was a seventeen-year-old high-school senior with only seventy days left until graduation. "The whys are relentless," says Trish, recalling endless days and nights of tears, loneliness, rage, and shame. There were also times when she questioned her faith. "As a parent, the guilt of outliving a child is horrifying," she says. "I was through with a God who lets children suffer and die. Now I realize that my faith was very small."[15]

Trish admits she continues to struggle on a daily basis with whys and guilt. She knows only one way to find peace to get through the day—she prays, focusing on the cross and on heaven.

"A pastor who counseled me in the second year of grief said, 'If you can't forgive yourself, then Jesus should have suffered more on Good Friday. He died for all sins of all times on that cross. Do you think He needs to suffer more?' I was angry and humbled at his words, but a light shone through them," Trish said.

Today, Trish realizes she will never know the answers to why her daughter had to battle depression and anorexia, why fourteen months of inpatient-outpatient treatment was unsuccessful, why prayers for healing and recovery went unanswered, and why, in Dawn's final days, she couldn't see the depth of her daughter's despair and hopelessness. "Memories still come back to haunt me," she says. "The devil just never gives up; but God's love never leaves us either, even when we're unaware of His presence."

As long as you and I live in this fallen world that groans for release from the choke hold of disease, decay, death, weeds, and the devil, we will continue to ask why. We will search for a cause while we seek a cure. We will wonder why God permits us to suffer. And we will question our reason for being here.

But Trish knows the real test of faith is when the only answer is the one Jesus gave his disciples about the blind man—to bring glory to God (John 9). Unfortunately, that is not exactly the answer we really want to hear or the truth we want to see.

PRAYER PAUSE: *Heavenly Father, I know my grief is blinding me, and You are so convenient to blame. I wonder how my feeble faith can ever bring You glory. But loss has broken through my flimsy impression of You. Grant me peace in what I don't understand.*

It is a sign of strength, not of weakness,
to admit that you don't know all the answers.

JOHN P. LOUGHRANE

25. So God works everything for good, huh?

Yet the Lord longs to be gracious to you; he rises to show you compassion. For the Lord is a God of justice. Blessed are all who wait for him!

ISAIAH 30:18 NIV

Adversity of any kind can have a freezing effect on our soul, bringing faith to a standstill. We struggle to understand a God who allows bad things to happen to good people and then claims to work everything for good. As we try to reconcile the two, many of us will discover a God far beyond our understanding. Some of us will turn our backs on Him, like my friend Diane.

It has been over thirty years since I stood at the grave site watching the casket of her two-year-old daughter lowered into the earth. The air was chilly that bleak October morning. I was in my early twenties, unacquainted with loss and unable to tell my friend what she desperately wanted to know: *How can anything good come out of so much suffering?* When leukemia took away her little girl, a part of Diane left with her. I know that I was never the same. That day at the cemetery, when my faith stood still, I learned that pat answers and spiritual cliches are impotent.

So how do we reconcile our lives and our losses with this verse: "And we know that God causes everything to work together for the good of those who love God and are called according to his purpose for them" (Romans 8:28)? What good comes out of loss?

Author Philip Yancey, who has spent a lifetime researching and writing about this piercing topic, concludes: "Not until history has run its course will we understand how 'all things work together for good.' Faith means believing in advance what will only make sense in reverse." Yancey contrasts *our being trapped in time* with *God's goodness that exists outside of time*, and says, "We remain ignorant of many details, not because God enjoys keeping us in the dark, but because we have not the faculties to absorb so much light."[16]

I am reminded how my ignorance of horticulture almost wiped out a Thanksgiving cactus. The plant was loaded with reddish-orange blooms when I brought it home from the nursery, determined to turn it into a houseplant. After the flowers dropped and the stems drooped, I moved it outside next to a pot of geraniums and watered like crazy. In disbelief, I watched the cactus rot while the geraniums thrived.

Then, I read a book on cacti and learned that what I had thought was *good for that specific cactus* wasn't. Instead of liking moist soil, this tree dweller needed to dry out between waterings. Native to tropical jungles in Central and South America and parts of Mexico, the *Schumbergera bridgesii* grows best in cool night temperatures, not in a hothouse environment or freezing winter fog. To cultivate blossoms, I had to lay aside my preconceptions and submit to a biological process that I still don't fully understand—that particular cactus required a six- to eight-week rest period in an unheated area with little light or water.[17]

Our lives are like that. The things we think are good for us may not be. Sometimes it takes a loss to bring us back to what matters, to drive us onto our knees and into the Book. It may take weeks or months of sitting slumped in a dark place before we are ready to be brought into the light where we can bloom again. Try as we might to make sense of our circumstances, we will not fully understand the whole scope of God's plan until we get to heaven. Only then, when our earthly tears are history and our life is in harmony with His ideal, will the *good* we yearn for be completely known.

For now, *good* is getting through this moment; then, the next.

It is surviving today; then, tomorrow, knowing deep in our roots daylight will come. *Good* is glancing back at yesterday and realizing God always intervenes. He takes the past and redeems it, and He permits loss to wise us up. *Good* is any occasion in which we can lay aside our preconceptions about life and loss and dare to believe "that God, who began the good work within you, will continue his work until it is finally finished on that day when Christ Jesus comes back again" (Philippians 1:6).

PRAYER PAUSE: *Lord, help me believe that You never sanction or promote evil in my life; that You are always looking out for my best interest—even when You work through adversity to accomplish it; and that You have already weighed my needs and prepared the solution.*

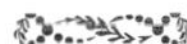

Once you become aware
that the main business you are here for
is to know God,
most of life's problems fall into place of their own accord.

J. I. PACKER

26. *The times when it's tough to praise Him*

Even though . . . fig trees have no blossoms, . . . no grapes on the vine, . . .
olive crop fails, . . . fields lie empty and barren, . . .
flocks die, . . . cattle barns are empty,
yet I will rejoice in the Lord! I will be joyful in the God of my salvation.

HABAKKUK 3:17-18

How easily we talk about faith when times are prosperous and our bodies are healthy. How loudly we sing those praise choruses when the refrigerator is stocked with food and we are surrounded by the love of family and friends. But when the situation changes and our prayers go unanswered, praising God gets tough.

Some of us have the misconception that we need to be in a light-hearted frame of mind to praise God. But do you know that praise is independent of method or mood? It does not mean we pretend gratitude or deny grief. Proverbs describes the negative effect of cheerful songs on a heavy heart.[18] Praise means adoring God with a whole heart in spite of our circumstances or how we feel. It is an act of worship. John 4:23-24 tells us that God seeks our praise and that we are to worship Him "in spirit and in truth."

During loss and adversity, most of us, if we would admit it, struggle to praise God. David wrote more psalms of lament than of praise. I imagine the men and women of faith, who are mentioned in the eleventh chapter of Hebrews, had occasions when they struggled. Their life experiences were not conducive to a merry mood or lighthearted frame of mind. They died before ever receiving what God had promised them. Some were tortured for their faith; others, mocked and whipped. Several were stoned, sawed in half, or gored with a sword. Many went hungry.

Philip Yancey describes such faith as *fidelity faith*. It is faith that hangs on at any cost, when miracles do not come, and prayers go unanswered, and when "nothing works according to formula and all of the Bible's promises seem glaringly false."[19] This is the faith of Job who said, "Though He slay me, I will hope in Him" (Job 13:15 NASB).

The story of Abraham not only demonstrates fidelity faith but the worship of God in spite of circumstances or feelings. After God told him to sacrifice Isaac, Abraham put his whole heart into the journey—a decision based not on wild enthusiasm but sincere devotion and earnest commitment. Obediently, he trudged to the top of Mount Moriah, built an altar, stoked it with wood, tied up his son, and laid him on top. Then, he pulled out his knife and lifted it up to kill the child for whom he had waited so long, unaware an angel would intervene with an animal sacrifice and God would spare his son (Genesis 22).

A friend of mine knows the cost of such fidelity faith. When her husband was diagnosed with a deadly brain tumor, people flooded her with calls and notes saying they knew he would be healed, and my friend believed it was true. However, after a barrage of painful medical procedures, surgery, radiation, and no miracle, her husband said, "It's hard to see God as a loving Father in all this." She agreed. Later that day, while alone in the car, she finally began to grieve the grueling ordeal. She described groaning from the pit of her stomach as she gave God permission to do whatever He had to do. "I chose once again to love, trust, obey, and serve Him," she said, "even if in this life, this pain is all there is, with no future to make up for it, no weight of glory to look forward to."

In these soul-searching moments, when rafter-raising choruses are far from our lips and groaning is all we have left to give,

God accepts our wholehearted praise. Praise is more than a thrilling emotional response to an inspirational message. Whether it flows from delight or rises from the depths of sorrow, authentic praise is an act of our will. Adoring God does not mean we need to feel a spiritual high or be sitting in a sanctuary pew. Praise also takes place in everyday moments during our spiritual lows as we faithfully live out our ordinary lives.[20]

PRAYER PAUSE: *Lord God, laying my body, mind, and spirit into Your hands is going to take some doing. I know obedience is the way to genuine joy—that deep, settled confidence that You are in control. But for now, all I can offer is gratitude that You are acquainted with my grief.*

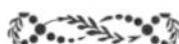

I am convinced that He leads us into situations that are impossible to face without Him.

LLOYD JOHN OGILVIE

27. Faith to doubt and still believe God is really there

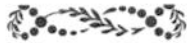

When doubts filled my mind,
your comfort gave me renewed hope and cheer.

PSALM 94:19

There is an intriguing tale about a shipwreck and its sole survivor, a man who was washed up on a small, uninhabited island. He desperately prayed for God to rescue him. Every day he scanned the horizon for help, but no one came. As he waited, he searched for driftwood and built a small hut for protection from the elements and for storage of his meager possessions.

One day, after scavenging for food, he arrived at his hut and found it in flames, with huge plumes of smoke coiling toward the sky. Everything was lost! He could not imagine anything worse. With his faith shaken, he abandoned all hope that he would ever be rescued. Breaking down, he angrily cried out to God: "How could you do this to me!"

After a fitful night, he awoke to the rumble of an approaching ship. He watched it drop anchor and launch a raft toward shore. "How did you know I was here?" he asked his rescuers.

"We saw your smoke signal!" they replied.

It is easy to become discouraged and doubt God when our circumstances take an unexpected turn and loss incinerates our dreams. But in the ashes of our lives, God is at work. He is never more present and we are never more open and available to Him.

When we seek the face of God in prayer, like the survivor in this story, we consciously affirm that God sees, He hears, He is. Praying is more than presenting requests to God. It is listening and waiting—being willing to be changed in relationship to Him.

Prayer transforms us in physical ways that medical science is only beginning to understand. Research reveals that prayer promotes longevity and reduces an unhealthy plaque buildup in the carotid artery. "A part of prayer's effect might come from removing stress—reversing that burst of hormones that can suppress immune-cell function," says Ellen Sternberg, a leading researcher on the link between the brain and immune system for the National Institute of Health.[21] Duke University researcher Harold Koenig, a family physician whose observations of patients praying or reading Scripture led him to investigate religion's impact on health, reached a similar conclusion following a six-year study of 4,000 senior citizens.[22]

Here's a level of stress you probably haven't reached yet—imagine waking up in a body bag after being pronounced dead. Up until the eulogy, Theresa had led a rather unspiritual and materialistic life; then prayer transformed the spiritual life of this young Castilian woman, Theresa of Avila. She was born in 1515, ironically, the same year that Martin Luther posted the Ninety-five Theses that launched the Protestant Revolution. As a young woman, Theresa suddenly developed a mysterious illness some scholars speculate was epilepsy or narcolepsy. After being left for burial at a local convent and later reviving, she joined a Carmelite order known for its practice of prayer handed down from early Christians who had built retreats on Mount Carmel in Palestine.

Theresa's writings reveal that she felt lukewarm toward God and often spent her daily hour of prayer watching the hourglass, wishing it would end. Although she described those years of spiritual reluctance as the most miserable of her life, she also said she found greater stability and peace during those reluctant times where she trained herself to pray than in rapturous times of great emotion and excitement.[22]

As Theresa of Avila discovered, ambivalent or lukewarm feelings are not the death-knell of faith but a summons to enter into an honest relationship with God. Perhaps our most authentic prayers are arguments, as we seek to understand life's ambiguities and God for who He is, rather than for what He can give us.

PRAYER PAUSE: *Almighty God, thank you for the faith to doubt and still believe You are really there. When my life is reduced to ashes, may I fear nothing but the loss of You.*

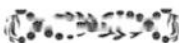

The feeling remains that God is on this journey too.

THERESA OF AVILA

28. Almighty God, meet me in this hour.

But I called on your name, Lord,
from deep within the well, and you heard me!
You listened to my pleading; you heard my weeping!
Yes, you came at my despairing cry and told me, "Do not fear."

LAMENTATIONS 3:55-57

Sometimes the spiritual darkness of loss is impenetrable. We feel like a frightened child who has fallen into a deep well. It seems God has abandoned us in our hour of need, when we have sunk to the bottom. In fear, we cry out like the psalmist David, "I have been cut off from the Lord!" (Psalm 31:22).

This fear is especially acute if we are the children of divorce, who have grown up without a father. Our template for a committed relationship has collapsed around us. Because we are unable to trust our earthly father, we are afraid to trust our heavenly one and worry that He has given up on us, too. Without a stable family structure or hope for the future, life looks bleak.

"Being an adult child of divorce can sometimes make it difficult for us either to recognize our spiritual needs or to make use of our spiritual resources," says Dr. Archibald Hart, former dean of Fuller Theological Seminary's Graduate School of Psychology. Hart, who grew up in a divorced family, believes divorce not only strikes at the core of children's fundamental need for stability and security, but it also distorts their view of God, which "tends to keep [them] at a distance from the Source of all healing."[24]

An acquaintance of mine says growing up without a father brought her closer to God. "My father left when I was ten; and now in his nineties, he's still chasing women. He was a preacher who ran off with a gal in the congregation," she said. "Because divorce wasn't common in those days, my mother lived under its shadow." Although my friend longed for a father's love, she learned that God uses loss to make something beautiful. Recently, she found herself weeping while watching a television documentary on dead-beat dads. "I realized that nobody ever taught those children that they had a heavenly Father who loves them," she said, crediting her mother, who without job skills or support started a faith mission to migrant farm workers. "Mother taught my brother and me that when we needed food, we went to our knees. We knew our next meal was coming from our heavenly Father."

Has your view of God been distorted by divorce or a parent's critical nature? Do you feel stuck in a spiritual black hole, struggling with the fear that God has given up on you? Voice your fears and frustrations to God. He longs to show you a correct image of who He is: faithful and true, loving and merciful, almighty and holy—the God who keeps His promises.

Envision His outstretched hands and your name tattooed on His palms (Isaiah 49:16). Know that nothing can separate you from your Father in heaven—not death, divorce, an earthly father's abandonment, or the desertion of family and friends (Romans 8:35). Take comfort in Psalm 27:10—"Even if my father and mother abandon me, the Lord will hold me close."

PRAYER PAUSE: *God, I long to trust You as Father, but I'm afraid. No one has ever shown me what lasting love or a committed relationship looks like. Show me the stability of Your lasting love.*

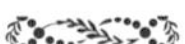

I know God won't give me much more than I can handle.
I just wish He didn't trust me so much.

MOTHER TERESA

My Mini Journal of Hope and Gratitude

. . . I will never forsake you. HEBREWS 13:5

DATE	MY DOUBTS AND QUESTIONS	GOD'S "RIGHT NOW"

If you are wondering what God is up to in your life, you can probably empathize with Israel's former prime minister, Golda Meir, who said: "Moses dragged us for forty years through the desert to bring us to the one place in the Middle East where there was no oil."

Dear God,
Instead of letting people die and having to make new ones, why don't you just keep the ones you have now?
—Jane

LETTER FROM A CHILD
(SOURCE: INTERNET)

Pivotal Moments

Sandwiched Between Solitary and Ordinary Days

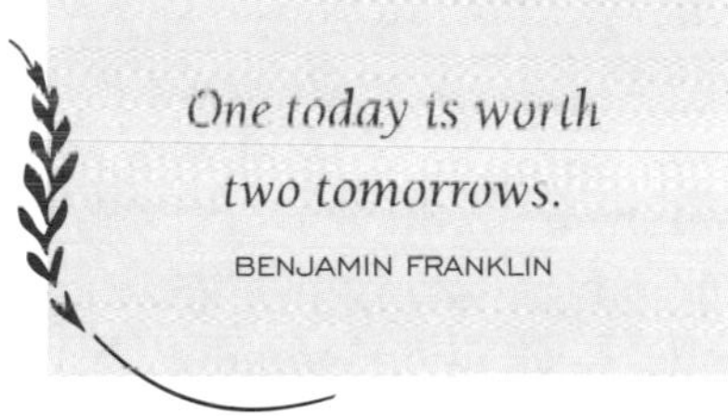

One today is worth
two tomorrows.
BENJAMIN FRANKLIN

29. *After the mourners leave*

O God . . . my soul thirsts for you; my whole body longs for you in this parched and weary land where there is no water. . . . I lie awake thinking of you, meditating on you through the night. I think how much you have helped me; . . . your strong right hand holds me securely.

PSALM 63:1, 6-8

There are pivotal moments in each of our lives that change us forever. They happen when you come upon a particular phrase in a poem that inspires you to think differently. Or when someone tells a good joke and you realize you haven't laughed in a long time. It happens when you go through a certain phase of life and recognize a truth that has eluded you before. You feel these pivotal moments when someone is born, when you fall in love, or when someone dies. Some of us, at the core of our being, recognize the immutable impact of these moments the instant they occur and will draw from them years later. I know.

I was a freshman in high school by the time I finally had an opportunity to spend a week at my grandmother's. We had moved from California to Colorado, making the drive to Grandma's Nebraska home manageable. A widow in her early sixties with no source of income, she earned Social Security credits by opening her home to eighty- and ninety-year-old boarders. In the evenings, with the chores finished, we retreated to her small attic bedroom, which was perfumed with rose water and homemade peanut brittle. We talked for hours, often past midnight.

During one of our chats, I remarked about a collection of rather large, brightly colored satin ribbons tucked into a vase in the far corner. My grandmother explained that they were all that remained of the flower arrangements at my grandfather's funeral. She said, "They were just too pretty to toss out."

My memory of Grandfather's death is through the eyes of a young child. I recall my mother receiving a phone call and the next minute she was crying. We had lived too far away to attend, so I now wanted to know all about it. My grandmother showed me a stack of beautiful sympathy cards, and she shared how friends came to the house bearing casseroles.

I knew that faith held Grandma together, but I wondered how she survived that day. "Oh, the day of the funeral isn't what gets you," Grandma said. "That day you have lots of company. What gets you is the next day, after all the mourners leave."

That night as I snuggled beneath a hand-appliqued butterfly quilt, I could *almost* imagine what it must have felt like to be left alone. That moment was pivotal for me. I'd remember it years later as I lived out a similar, yet different, loss, drawing strength from my grandmother's experience to face my own aloneness.

Most of us abhor aloneness, yet we are often powerless to avoid it. Loss forces this vacuous emptiness upon us. When the well-wishers stop sending cards and bringing casseroles, we confront it. Here, we discover who we really are when no one is looking. Hidden between solitary and ordinary days are opportunities to forge an identity less dependent upon the externals.

PRAYER PAUSE: *Heavenly Father, You have been with me in the past, but I need to sense Your hand on my life right now. Help me believe that just as You are more powerful than the wind and sea, You are also more powerful than the forces of aloneness that I face today.*

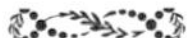

The things which hurt, instruct.

BENJAMIN FRANKLIN

30. When friends don't understand

Do not stay so far from me, for trouble is near, and no one else can help me.

PSALM 22:11

Are you discovering a lot of your friends just don't seem to get it? For a while, they may listen intently as you tell your story. Some leave encouraging messages on your answering machine. Maybe one will say, "I'm here for you. Call anytime." A few even drop by to see how you are coping—for a while. But eventually, most of them succumb to the typical refrain: *Get on with it. Get over it. Get a life.*

The problem is not you. This does not mean that you are doing something wrong, or that you are taking too much time to work through your losses. Unless it has happened to them, most people don't have a clue about what we go through when a mate, a marriage, or a loved one dies. They are able to intellectualize concepts such as every marriage ends either by death or divorce and every person dies either in youth, middle age, or old age. But not for a single moment have they personally stood in the pool of tears where you now stand. They have never felt the interminable aloneness of a room filled only with memories. No wonder they cannot understand!

Consider yourself fortunate if you have even one person you can count on. Friends like this are there for the long haul. They continue inviting you to dinner even after all the times you refuse. Not only do they include you in their family, but they involve you in life again. Be comforted knowing that such a friend is there for you.

The rest of us can take comfort knowing that we are not abandoned, even if it feels or looks that way. The rejection we sense may not be deliberate; it may emanate from others' busyness or need to keep pain at a safe distance.

You see, to come alongside a friend who is grieving means you have to step beyond your comfort zone. First, you must acknowledge that the world is not a safe place and that people suffer. Next, you must be willing to enter into their pain. For whatever reason, not everyone has this capacity. Don't take it personally. This is not about you. Empathy is something not everyone can give.

In the meantime, lean into these shifts in your relationships. Others' lack of consolation or assistance may not be permanent. Right now they may be unable to take on your pain or concerns because they are coping with their own. Do not hesitate to seek the help you need from a support group.

Learning that it's okay to speak of your pain without expecting something in return is a pivotal moment you can carry with you, to help you now and improve future relationships. It does not lessen the truth you are telling or invalidate what you are going through. You are beginning the necessary struggle of standing upright on your own without needing others' approval or applause.

PRAYER PAUSE: *Lord Jesus, I know You understand. I think about Your time of greatest need in the Garden of Gethsemane, and I realize that even Your disciples left You.*

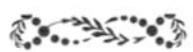

Men are not against you;
they are merely for themselves.

GENE FOWLER

31. Sitting alone in the pew

Even if my father and mother abandon me, the Lord will hold me close.

PSALM 27:10

I feel so alone and out of place. I'm trying to find what it is God wants of me, but I'm not sure what to do," says Donna Caraway, describing the unexpected end of her marriage. "I've talked to the pastor at my church, and I just don't think he gets it. I try to explain my feelings, but he doesn't know what to say or do. If I weren't the only piano player they had, I'd be gone!" Donna is not the only one noticing the hardness of the pew, the awkward glances, or the vacant seat next to her. Women across the country write me about similar situations that validate my own experience when I became single again. If your situation is like mine, you may be the only one in your family who is divorced. If you are like Donna, you may be the only divorced person in your church. Or maybe you are recently widowed. Perhaps you never married, like my friend Shari in Colorado. For whatever reason you find yourself sitting alone in your pew each week— it's time to advertise that prime real estate beside you.

"I am disappointed with how the church handles career singles, separating us like we are a tribe of our own. We like to mix with children and couples like everybody else," says Shari. "I finally realized that I truly enjoy the companionship of couples, and it is okay to do things with couples." After teaching adult Sunday school classes and Bible studies in her local church, she befriended several couples and discovered she likes hearing men pray. "Men pray differently than women," Shari adds. "I enjoy the way they look at the world and the things they talk about."

Peggy, divorced and living in Kansas City, Missouri, credits her brother, who is pastor of her church, with integrating singles into the congregation. "I would prefer doing things with somebody I'm in love with," she says, "but since that's not possible now, I decided to start mingling with couples and seniors."

Whatever you decide to do about sitting alone in the pew, do not slink off without speaking to someone. You belong in the family of God as much as that newly married couple draped around each other in the back pew or the children skipping down the aisle. Your congregation needs you and you need them. Get vocal. Talk to the pastor. If he doesn't hear your concerns, attend board meetings. Or get creative, like Mary MacDonald in California, who organized monthly church potlucks that included four couples and one single. She called the groups "Supper for 9."

Many married congregation members are perplexed over how to relate to you, too. Some feel threatened by your singleness. They might keep you at arm's length to protect their territory, because they are afraid you are after their husbands. Why not invite them into your home for a cup of tea to discuss your deep longing to belong and their unspoken concerns? Then, the next time you meet in the sanctuary, they'll feel more comfortable saving you a seat. And you'll feel more comfortable taking it.

PRAYER PAUSE: *Father, I see couples everywhere—holding hands in the mall, strolling through airports, and dining out. It hurts. But I never thought I would feel this invisible in my own church. Help me to stop saying, "They don't include me." Help me to start saying, "I'm part of God's family. There's room for me here, too."*

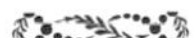

Don't leave before the miracle happens.

ANONYMOUS

32. *Accepting my vulnerability*

Through each day the Lord pours his unfailing love upon me, and through each night I sing his songs, praying to God who gives me life.

PSALM 42:8

"Why does everything hurt, when you know it's truly over and you are willing to let go, but your heart won't?" Becky, who lives in Georgia, asked in a recent e-mail. She described last December fifteenth, when she sat in her lawyer's office completing the final paperwork that would end her twenty-seven-year marriage and wondered why her husband so adamantly wanted the divorce before Christmas. A week later, she knew. As her ex-husband gathered the rest of his belongings from the family home, he let it slip that he was moving in with "his lady friend."

Like a rusty crow bar, unexpected betrayal pries open our hearts leaving us susceptible to deep wounds we never dreamed of and outside influences we never imagined. We are defenseless against what we never saw coming, do not understand, and cannot change. We flounder helplessly for a plausible explanation. When we feel exposed before a probing world, we are the most vulnerable. We long for somebody to protect us and make everything all right.

"I felt so overwhelmed by my first holiday without him," Becky later wrote. "There are a couple guys who said they'd like to take me out when I'm ready, but even that doesn't make me happy."

In the months that followed, as she raised her daughters and worked through her grief, Becky asked God to close the door to men that she should not be involved with. She described "long-legged contestants" who came and went, some bearing roses and jewelry. Although Becky longed for someone special in her life, she learned to be careful and to pray over every situation. She says, "The Lord is giving me so much wisdom in watching over my heart."

Whether you face a betrayal like Becky's or you are coming to terms with your loved one's death, you know that quiver of vulnerability. You feel it if you are forced to relocate to a different house in a strange city or when you lose your health or another close relationship. It is that sense of neediness that accompanies change, injury, attack, and criticism.

Learning to accept your vulnerability and co-exist with loneliness is not easy. You wonder if you will remain this way forever. Most of us, when we feel vulnerable, want somebody's arms around us, reassuring us that we are okay and that we will be okay. Because we feel like half of something broken, we assume that we will find the wholeness, acceptance, and approval we long for if only we could find love again.

We forget that learning to live in the midst of deep longings and great loneliness does not diminish us but enlarges our capacity for life and love. The more we realize that God has not abandoned us, but unconditionally loves us and will give us what we need, the more acceptance we find in who we are instead of in who we are with. We begin to unearth the courage to examine why we are here, where we are going, and how we want to spend the rest of our lives. In this place of vulnerability, we discover that being alone can strengthen us and does not contain the terror we imagined. And we begin to like our own company.

PRAYER PAUSE: *Heavenly Father, I feel so needy. Hold me tight during these times I so long for another relationship to lean on. Stay* *close beside me during these solitary moments when I am vulnerable. I know that how I spend my time when I am alone speaks volumes about what I value. Whatever the future holds, I want only Your best.*

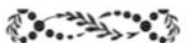

I do not believe that sheer suffering teaches.
If suffering alone taught,
then all the world would be wise, since everyone suffers.
To suffering must be added mourning, understanding,
patience, love, openness,
and the willingness to remain vulnerable.

ANNE MORROW LINDBERGH

33. *Hearing the sound of my own voice*

The Lord has heard the voice of my weeping.

PSALM 6:8 NASB

Ten years ago, we moved from sea level to the crest of the foothills. I remember the first day I walked into an overgrown field with a shovel and hoe in hand, determined to create a country garden. Standing in weeds up to my waist, I panned the string of homes under construction on the distant ridges and thought, *No one will hear me if I loose my balance and tumble down this steep slope.*

That day I figured my voice would simply ride the wind, sock the face of the cliffs, then plummet into the canyon below. In this somewhat lonesome landscape, that reflected my own doubts and fears at the time, I was flinching each time a lizard darted over my feet.

We all have these moments when we are convinced no one will hear us—whether our conviction comes from an inability to speak of unspeakable sorrow, fear of rejection, or negative self talk. We wonder if we have anything worthy to say. *Not another peep out of you! Stow it! Save your breath*, we have learned to tell ourselves. Soon we no longer hear the sound of our own voice. We are silenced at the very time we need to trust ourselves.

Former secretary-general of the United Nations Dag Hammarskjold once said, "The more faithfully you listen to the voice within you, the better you hear what is sounding outside of you."

Each one of us carries within us the truth about what we are experiencing and the discernment to sift through it. We know more than we think. However, we often discount the experiences for which we have paid dearly. We relegate them to nothing more than soundless footsteps in summer grass.

I believe God listens intently to these sounds of our heart, even the silent murmur of our discontent or the resonating doubt. Our Creator has an ear for our fears. He hears us sob in that place beyond tears. Romans 8:26-27 (NASB) speaks of God knowing what the Holy Spirit is saying when He prays for us with groanings "too deep for words." At the same time that God is witnessing the grief we cannot articulate, He is calling us to the life beyond it. He is the inner voice we hear.

In the outer world, there are many voices competing for our attention. Some edify, like the voices of caution and reason. A few distract and frighten us, like the voices of wild imaginings that fancy harmless lizards as poisonous snakes. Other voices create distortion.

If you grew up in or married into an abusive relationship, you may be hearing for the first time what was suppressed for a long time. In this pivotal moment, you are recognizing how your perception of the world around you was filtered through and controlled by others. Physical, emotional, and verbal abuse distort reality and can stifle your words, rendering you unable to speak. Sometimes such abuse pushes you to the edge. Now, without such background noise drowning out the truth and dragging you down into feelings and thoughts not of your making, you are picking up wisdom's frequency.

Our Creator designed us to tune our ears to wisdom. We are to "cry out for insight and understanding" and to pay attention when wisdom "calls out!" and "raises her voice!" summoning us onward to light and life (Proverbs 2:3; 8:1).

At a deep level, you have this inaudible yearning to reconnect with all that is living. You know the difference between how things are and how they appeared. With each breath you take and every beat of your heart, you are affirming the truth of what you have been through and what you have lost. In the process of listening to and telling yourself the truth, you are hearing your own voice.

PRAYER PAUSE: *Lord, with quiet astonishment I catch myself expressing gratitude for the lessons of loss. The more I confront my pain and fears without disguising them, the more I can verbalize what happened and how I am being changed in the process. Don't let the voice of truth fade or my ability to speak be silenced. Amplify Your presence within me and attune my heart to wisdom.*

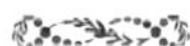

Death is not the greatest loss in life.
The greatest loss is what dies inside of us while we live.

NORMAN COUSINS

34. Forever changed by loss

Troubles and distress have come upon me,
but your commands are my delight.
. . . give me understanding that I may live.

PSALM 119:143, 144 NIV

Loss is the one common denominator that changes all our lives. We are never the same. Innocence is gone forever. We go on, but we don't laugh the way we used to. It is a catastrophic, life-altering event similar to a tornado, leaving in its wake ruthless devastation and disorientation. The world feels unsafe and the future, unsure.

"To go through one of these tornadoes is a psychological pummeling. It's really tough to get going, to make decisions, and time slips away from you like sand in an hourglass. You don't for a minute feel you're in charge," says Curtis Uhls, a survivor of the May 3, 1999 twister that tore through his neighborhood near Oklahoma City. Most of the red-brick ranch-style homes on the 380-yard-long block were leveled in the 318 mph winds.

Today, Curtis and his wife, Carol, one of the block's first families in the 1980s, are rebuilding on their leveled lot. While some residents feel added resolve, others battle anxiety when the sky darkens. Erma Gonzales says she bursts into tears driving down the street. "I'm not any less fearful of things generally; in fact, maybe more so," she says, "The difference is now I try not to let it hold me back.[25]

Neighbors Phyllis and Phil Halstead continue to look for his pioneer grandmother's iron kettle that she used to make lye soap. Annette Raiden, whose children rode out the tornado alone, continues to sift the rubble, but still can't find any evidence of the twenty-one Christmas ornaments she had purchased each holiday for every year of marriage. Annette longs to unearth a piece of her past. As Nina Shengold writes, "The objects we own remind us of who we are and, perhaps more important, who we have been. Our possessions are bread crumbs laid in a dark forest; we keep them to find our way home."[26]

As a tornado disintegrates everything in its path, loss disintegrates your concept of self, altering your view of the world and how you see your place in it. Death crushes dreams of what might have been. Divorce shatters everything you believed and valued, hoped for, and trusted in. Parenting patterns change. Your financial situation shifts—as does your social life and status in the community. If you are widowed or divorced, you are no longer someone's wife. Loss can also alter the way you look at the church, as you question the principles you have been taught and wonder where you fit. Since loss brings stress, it changes your body and your feelings about it. No wonder you sense that something is different. You *are* different. You are rapidly changing. Some days you change your attitude the way you switch lipsticks or alter your hairstyle.

As you look at the changes in your own life and sift through the remnants, you are mourning not only what you have lost but the person you no longer are. Like a tornado victim sifting through the rubble of a house, you are taking inventory of what is gone and what is left.

You may not know it yet, but this is a pivotal moment. You are looking for pieces to hold on to, much like you would search for chips of precious heirloom china. It is not so much that you can't let go, but that this is how we bury what's dead. We sort through our memories. One by one we turn them over in our minds. If we can say "This part was good. Here, I did my best.

Now it's time to grow a new life and rebuild," we bring meaning to our losses and value to our lives.

PRAYER PAUSE: *I'm such a creature of habit, Lord. I prefer the predictable to the changeable. Help me realize that it is not what happens to me in life that counts. What matters is how I respond to what happens and what I do with it. Show me how to appreciate this new evolving .me. I offer You my willingness to be changed forever.*

Forever is but a trail of "Nows."
The best a man can do is live every one fully in its turn.

AUTHOR UNKNOWN

35. Lord, with You beside me, I can do this.

I can never escape your spirit! I can never get away from your presence!
. . . if I go down to the place of the dead, you are there.
. . . I could ask the darkness to hide me and the light around me
to become night—but even in darkness I cannot hide from you. To you the
night shines as bright as day. Darkness and light are both alike to you.

PSALM 139:7, 8, 11-12

". . . The experience of loss itself does not have to be the defining moment in our lives. Instead, the defining moment can be our response to the loss," writes Gerald Sittser, associate professor of religion at Whitworth College in Spokane, Washington.[27] He knows what he is talking about. One dark night on a rural road in Idaho, a drunk driver rammed head-on into the van Sittser was driving, killing his wife, mother, and a four-year-old daughter. Alone, he watched them die.

"I remember the realization sweeping over me," he says, "that I would soon plunge into a darkness from which I might never again emerge as a sane, normal, believing man."[28]

Like Gerald Sittser, in your own encounter with loss, you are discovering both its terror and its transformation. You know that bad things do happen, that not everybody plays by the rules, and that good people can make wrong choices you are powerless to change. You also know that life is more random than fair and that you don't always receive a good review from your critics. Such recognition is a charged moment that makes you leap out of your seat to look for the nearest exit.

But instead of escaping, you are choosing to embrace the loss and suffering; and you are unknowingly encountering its life-altering transformation. The realization that you can decide the direction of your heart even though you cannot reverse what happened is a pivotal moment. How you choose to respond to your loss, or whether you respond at all, can rearrange your point of view and transfigure or worsen the harshest reality.

Gerald Sittser says catastrophic loss taught him "the incredible power of choice."[29] He found that the choice to enter the darkness does not mean any of us can, should, or do completely come out the other side. Instead, he found it a place where he learned to integrate the pain of loss into his life, to gain wisdom, and to grow in character. In the process, he became more sensitive to others' pain and more aware of darkness in the world around him.

With God beside us, you and I can also make the passage from where we are in our own dark, lonely night, to what we have in us to become. But that doesn't mean we will never feel uneasy or be unhappy. I have to admit I often react to my losses instead of choosing a response. I'm glad that's where grace steps in. Perhaps faith is exercised not only in moments of quiet resignation but also in thrusting our fist toward the heavens, and, like Job, seeking the answer to *Why?*

PRAYER PAUSE: *Heavenly Father, I despise loss. And I hate how it makes me feel. Unsure of myself. Vulnerable. Alone. When life spirals out of control like this, and I am unable to do anything about any of it, I want to run. But I have come so far! In my heart, I know the only way out of this wasteland is through it. With You beside me, I know I can do this. Help me see that loss hasn't obliterated my life and that the best may be waiting in all the moments yet to be.*

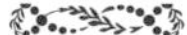

Life can only be understood backwards; but it must be lived forwards.

SOREN KIERKEGAARD

My Mini Journal of Hope and Gratitude

Lord, sustain me as you promised, that I may live! PSALM 119:116

DATE	WHAT I MISS THE MOST	WHAT I ALWAYS HAVE

Life comes in clusters, clusters of solitude, then clusters when there is hardly time to breathe

MAY SARTON

Creating Your Own Extraordinary Day

- Seize a lonely moment as an opportunity to listen to your favorite piece of music that nobody else can stand. Turn up the volume! Kick up your heels and howl!
- Order flowers delivered to your office addressed to yourself with a card reading: "Someone who cares about you."
- Call your pastor for the names of three women who recently lost a loved one and invite them to lunch after church on Sunday. Agree to meet once a month to sit together during the service and for potluck or restaurant fare afterwards.
- Eat chocolate!

Unavoidable Moments

For Sorting the Past and Savoring the Present

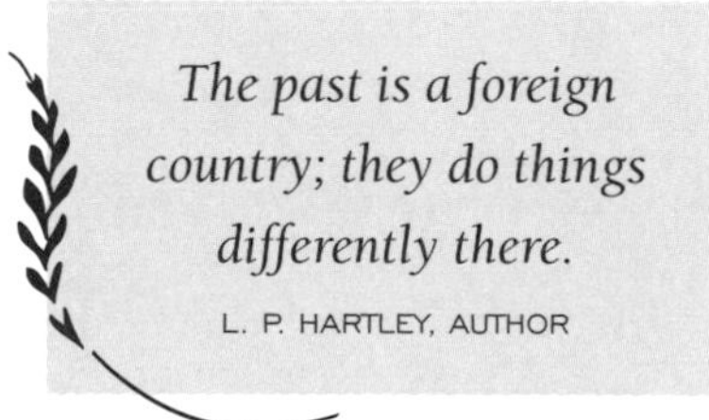

The past is a foreign country; they do things differently there.

L. P. HARTLEY, AUTHOR

36. The priceless family photos

O Lord, I will honor and praise your name, for you are my God.
You do such wonderful things! You planned them long ago,
and now you have accomplished them.

ISAIAH 25:1

We owe it to ourselves to remember the important events and experiences of our lives. They are the history of what has shaped us into the people we are today. Whenever we erase the parts that contribute to the whole, even if the memories are unhappy ones, we erase what is fully our unique selves.

I remember the day I could finally say that the dusty photograph albums stacked in the storage room were not about *who I was*, but priceless evidence of *who I am*. Earlier that week the fireplace insert in our bedroom had caught fire inside the chimney. There was smoke damage that required repainting and cleaning. As I reorganized my closet, I discovered a couple of scarves and belts left over from the early days of my first marriage. But I was not prepared for the emotions my discovery unleashed.

Even though I had put the divorce behind me and was four years into a very happy second marriage, the tears started. That day I wept not because I still loved my ex-husband but because I was reconnecting with a part of me that was missing. The feeling was one of being lost, then finding my way home.

You see, for too long I had relegated to the past *that woman* who peered out of years of fading snapshots in those dusty albums. She had been packed away in the divorce. She was too naive and trusting. Since I no longer recognized her as myself, I erased her existence with the label *who I was*.

That day on the floor of my closet, I found her. "No!" I shrieked aloud. "This is not about *who I was*. The woman who wore these scarves and belts is *who I am*." Soon I had gathered two decades of albums together, spread them out across the family room carpet, and was turning the pages one by one, searching, laughing, and sighing. When my teenager arrived home from school, I walked her through the pages of our lives. "Remember that rabbit cake I baked for your birthday?" I asked. "And here we are having a tea party with your Cabbage Patch dolls." That evening I flipped through the albums with my new husband. "This is how I looked at 25," I said. "This suit, that sweater, and those drapes . . . I made them!" In black and white and in living color, Richard saw that the middle-aged woman he married had *always* loved to garden. And I saw that the history I had once shared with my ex-husband contributed to the woman I am today.

Within your own life story, there is a unique love story—of father-mother-child love, a first love, a betrayed or rekindled love, or of a love lost. It is written out of the history you shared with a loved one now gone. Whether you are a widow with memories that are good, or a divorcee with memories that are an odd mix, you owe it to yourself to remember. Each time you draw strength from the events and experiences that have shaped your life, you link the past to the present and become a little more whole.

PRAYER PAUSE: *Lord, as I flip through photographs, I thank You for life and for the opportunity to love and be loved. I'm grateful that no one can take away my memories. I also know that I left a part of me behind, too—in the lives I touched and the flower beds I planted.*

We ask for long life, but 'tis deep life, or grand moments, that signify.

RALPH WALDO EMERSON

37. *Precious trinkets and the wedding album*

You won't let me sleep. I am too distressed even to pray! I think of the good old days, long since ended, when my nights were filled with joyful songs. I search my soul and think about the difference now.

PSALM 77:4-8

When you spend thirty years of your life learning to love you get to be pretty good at it. Then one day you wake up and realize that most of the people you loved in your life are grown or gone," writes award-winning columnist Sharon Randall, who was recently widowed. She describes how "sitting in an empty family room with a house full of scrapbooks, five sets of dishes, and this enormous capacity for love" isn't such a bad place to be if you can figure out what to do with it.[30]

If your spouse passed away, as Sharon's did, or left you in a divorce, or if someone you loved died, one of your most difficult tasks is figuring out what to do with the images and tokens of a love now gone. The cedar chest with the baby's nightgowns. A toddler's favorite bunny. Your teenager's high-school class ring. They are reminders of a child's life cut short and a future that will never be. That wedding album. Maybe a diamond engagement ring. Your gold band. These emblems symbolize not only another's promise but that once you were his wife. The album chronicles the day you and your fiancé stood before God and witnesses, vowing fidelity, promising lifelong love, becoming man and wife.

If you have lost this one who knew your heart as no other did, emotions you thought you had dealt with may rise again to the surface whenever you encounter these emblems. If you sense you aren't ready to make a decision about your ring or to pore over the photographs, it's okay. When the time is right, you'll know. Then, blinking tears back through wet lashes, you will walk again down love's aisle, remembering the moment you said, "Yes, I'll marry you" and recalling the day you said, "I do."

Some of you can already say, "I'm glad we had photographs taken. They remind me of that happy day and the dreams of the life we would have together." You keep the album on the bookshelf to show the grandchildren. You treasure your ring. You aren't ready to take it off.

Others might say, as I did, "I can't stand to look at this album; it makes me sad." Maybe you also wonder, "Was he lying to me then?" You slam the album shut and hurl it out of sight. As you rip the ring off your finger and toss it in the junk drawer, you feel cheated. Like every other bride, you once treasured these symbols of a marriage you thought would last a lifetime. Now you know it was not to be. You wonder if it ever was what you thought. You rail at the emotional price you've paid. Not only has the one you loved betrayed you, but his deception has trashed your memories, too. While this is a different loss than widows face, it is one you must begin to grieve.

Whatever or whoever you have lost, don't be afraid; rather, be encouraged that somewhere in the grieving process you will figure out what to do with those trinkets. Take all the time you need. You'll know when it is time to rummage through the layers of your cedar chest. You will hug the ear-chewed bunny, and it will tug your heart back to the precious moments it represents. You'll either savor the memories or reconcile with the emblems of your marriage.

If you divorced, in time, you will retrieve that gold ring and view it as evidence that you were not a failure, that you were the one who took those vows seriously. Then, you'll flip through that wedding album just as widows do. You will look into the eyes of the woman you were before the wound and recognize that the love and trust you pledged are not your faults but your gifts. These character qualities are who you are at the core of your being. They are patterned after God's own heart. That moment of realization is one you will forever savor.

PRAYER PAUSE: *Heavenly Father, this wedding album weighs heavy in my hands. So much has happened between now and then that I hardly recognize myself in the photos. How I long for the love I've lost. Stay with me while I sort through these emblems of my past. In those moments when I don't think I can stand the pain, remind me it is only because they symbolize something very precious to me.*

It is not so much what we have done amiss,
as what we have left undone, that troubles us, looking back.

ELLEN WOOD, PLAYWRIGHT

38. *Those birthdays and death days*

You saw me before I was born.
Every day of my life was recorded in your book.
Every moment was laid out before a single day had passed.

PSALM 139:16

I buried my son the day before his birthday," recalls Virginia Wainwright. "The last time I talked to Joey was nine-thirty Saturday night when he called saying to expect him home for his birthday." Virginia, a hospital intensive care nurse in Northern California, was off work that Sunday morning when someone knocked on her door. She thought the neighbors were complaining about her dogs. Instead, it was the police with news that her son had been in a car accident. He had died instantly. "In that moment all the color went out of the sky," She says. "That entire time period is all jammed together. To this day I remember the day of Joey's death more than I do his birthday. I can't isolate it."

Like Virginia, you may find that your concept of time blurs. At first, you don't think the loss is real. But the instant you grasp that the bond is permanently severed, you know it will be impossible to forget *that day*. Now, without even realizing it, you chronicle time from the date of loss—*It has been five years since she passed away. Eleven years ago he died. My mother would have been ninety-four,* or as Virginia says, *"Joey would be thirty-two now."*

Virginia says for two to three years after her son's death she took off work the entire week between his death day and birthday because the memory was so gruesome. Over time she learned not to dwell on it, preferring to stay busy at home *that day* and go to bed early. "Because this was the tenth year, it was hard," she says.

"I went to the cemetery with my pastor and we had prayer. What I really wish is that people would call me on that day, but they don't—because they don't remember." However you choose to pay tribute to loved ones, whether their lives were cut short or fully lived, you may find that the days that once called for celebration, like birthdays, are linked to mourning. Your family, friends, and pastor may not always understand your need to remember. Some people remain afraid of your emotions. Others continue to change the subject because they are unable to speak the words *died* or *killed*. The rest will keep their distance. Over the years, you will find, as Virginia did, that many people just won't remember—but that does not mean you can't.

Pamela Kendall's family still remembers. This year they placed an ad in the newspaper featuring her picture. They honored her memory with this poem:

In Loving Memory of Pamela D. Kendall
January 29, 1957, to April 22, 1977

If tears could build a stairway, and memories were a lane
I'd walk right up to heaven to bring you home again.
No farewell words were spoken, no time to say good-bye
You were gone before I knew it, and only God knows why.
My heart still aches in sadness, and secret tears still flow;
What it's meant to lose you, no one will ever know.

Love, Mom Cullen; Sisters, Diane and Angie; Brothers, Otis and Bruce

PRAYER PAUSE: *Creator God, you are sovereign; You knew each day of my loved ones' lives before they were born. Thank you for adding them to my life so that I could love them. I'll never forget them.*

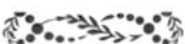

The way to love anything is to realize it might be lost.

G. K. CHESTERTON

39. *Anniversaries—past, present, future*

Don't long for the "good ole days,"
for you don't know whether they were any better than today.

ECCLESIASTES 7:10

Anniversaries commemorate a past event that we remember with celebration . . . or sadness. Some anniversaries are centennial, like the two hundredth anniversary of America's Independence Day. Others we remember annually, like the senseless shootings on April 20, 1999, at Columbine High School.

"All the grief and pain of this tragedy is bringing up unresolved losses in people's lives. When a lot of us were crying for the victims of Columbine, subconsciously we also might have been crying over losses we have never truly grieved," says Sandy Austin, a Columbine High School counselor. "If people did not work through the grief issues that were brought up at that time, then the anniversary will likely bring it up again."

Sandy's words speak to why that first anniversary of a loss is the hardest day to get through and why the anniversary of a special event we once shared with a loved one will forever be bittersweet. We cherish the memory of a wedding, graduation, or retirement along with a sad realization that each year that particular date rolls around, we will face the milestone alone. The more that day meant to us the greater our grief.

"An anniversary is a two-person event. A marriage starts it; a divorce or a death ends it," writes Jim Smoke, author, pastor, and adjunct professor. "Let the memories stand, but put them in the back of your mind and leave them there. You can't live at the crossroads of those memories. You must choose to move ahead."[31]

I remember receiving an invitation to friends' twenty-fifth anniversary party shortly after my ex-husband filed for divorce. I arrived, bearing a gift and wearing a smile; but inside I was coming apart at the seams. My marriage had ended three years short of such a celebration. I know widows who report similar feelings. After losing a spouse, the hullabaloo over someone's diamond or golden anniversary can make you cringe. The pastor's tribute to the couple married the longest becomes a bridge to a painful memory.

Suzanna, whom we've met in Chapter 5, shared, "As I write this, my former church is meeting at the steak house one-half mile from my house for the annual Valentine's Day banquet. He is there with her. And to top that off, just this week I received a wedding invitation from a young woman addressed to my ex-husband and me. How it broke my heart to send her a card along with a note telling her that we are divorced."

Anniversaries are as inevitable as the seasons. While they bring us full circle in our grief—reminding us of losses yet to mourn and milestones we will never reach—they also are life-giving. As we learn to live these unavoidable moments, we discover that none of us is immune to longing for what could have been, nor do we have to be indifferent to others' joy. Each time we are able to recall the past and be thankful that it happened at all, we revolutionize its meaning. And we celebrate life.

PRAYER PAUSE: *Lord, anniversaries are so painful. Yet I am grateful that I can still hold my loved ones in memory even after they are with You. When events reopen old wounds, may they teach me tenacity to keep living.*

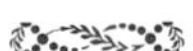

People only see what they are prepared to see.

RALPH WALDO EMERSON

40. *Thanksgiving—the grit about gratitude*

. . . I will present my thank offerings to you.
For you have delivered me from death and my feet from stumbling,
that I may walk before God in the light of life.

PSALM 56:12-13 NIV

Loss by its nature appears to take more from us than it gives. It shatters our expectations about life. Loss breaks hearts, rattles minds, fatigues bodies, and frustrates faith. We wrestle with biblical advice to *be thankful in all things* while we wrangle over how to *give thanks for such misery*.

Jeanne, from Arkansas, was told when she was a teenager that she had epilepsy and would need to take medication the rest of her life. "You want to scream, *'No! Just fix it!'*" she says, "It's so much like being betrayed by a husband, except you're betrayed by a body that is supposed to work for, not against, you."

Eight years after the diagnosis, while camping with her husband, Jeanne began to tally the things she was thankful for—time, wildlife, stars, her husband, the vacation, the camper. She was overwhelmed with thankfulness. "I became speechless," she says. "Taking a few lousy pills became such a little thing."

But *thankfulness in all things* is a lesson that needs to be dealt with again and again. Last summer, Jeanne and her husband renewed their vows in front of seventy family members and close friends to celebrate their twenty-fifth anniversary. She would soon learn her husband was sleeping with another woman and had even asked their daughter to invite the woman to the rededication party. Jeanne says, "I am a hospice nurse and watch people die daily, but it is nothing compared to this."

Like Jeanne, most of us struggle in normal circumstances to *be thankful in all things*. But when losses keep coming, we need a lot of grit to see reasons to be grateful. Now in the throes of an unwanted divorce, Jeanne says she tries to avoid pity parties because they leave no room for the uplifting—they shut out friends, loved ones, and God. She credits her mother with showing her and four siblings how to live with a grateful heart even in misery. In Jeanne's eyes, her mother stands tall despite crippling multiple sclerosis, which confines her to a wheelchair.

In the midst of whatever misery you and I face, sometimes all we can do to avoid loss getting the best of us is to look around and tally up what we have and what we always had. It is not because life is good that we thank God, but because He is good.

"I know it isn't Thanksgiving Day, but I have been thinking about the importance of living life with a grateful heart," Shari recently wrote. "I've been discouraged lately, so I began to list the ways God blesses me. What happened is amazing. Before I knew it, I was encouraged and focused on the trustworthy character of God." Here's a sampling of her list—being a child of God, the privilege and pleasure of prayer, love of family and friends, food and shelter, contributing to others' lives, laughter, music, living in this nation . . . each sunrise, sunset, and season.

PRAYER PAUSE: *Heavenly Father, my table has more empty chairs around it this year, and the faces at family celebrations have changed; but I am trying not to count my losses. I know I can count on You, because You never change.*

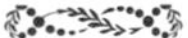

So often we try to alter circumstances to suit ourselves, instead of letting them alter us.

MOTHER MARIBEL

41. Christmas—breaking with tradition

. . . Nothing can ever separate us from his love.
Death . . . life . . . angels . . . demons can't.
Our fears for today, our worries for tomorrow,
and even the powers of hell can't keep God's love away.

ROMANS 8:38

Christmas is found in the heart, not under a tree. But when your heart is breaking and you are grieving, getting through this particular holiday can be rough. The season becomes more of a burden than a blessing. Wherever we turn, we see people trying to cram an old-fashioned, picture-perfect holiday into their hectic schedule. The frenzy is contagious. Haunted by our own Christmas Past, we start to feel left out. Our friends and family wonder why we just can't get into it anymore.

No wonder holiday blues light up crisis hot lines across the country and colds abound. Days shorten. Expectations lengthen. Stress increases. Stores are crowded; airports, jammed. We lose sleep. Some of us overeat; others, overbuy. We spend time with people we would rather not be with and miss loved ones who are deceased. Our depression mounts—along with the dread of reading piles of glowing newsletters from friends announcing fabulous vacations, great promotions, and their kids' grade point averages. No longer do we feel comfortable turning to them when we're down. After all, what happy family wants our sorrows? If our family was splintered in a divorce, we may harbor guilt and resentment as our children go to stay with their dad. We are angry that finances are low and there's no place to go.

If you add it all up, there isn't a better time to break with tradition. To stop searching for the right gift or that perfect tree. To stare through the mirage of holiday glitter and garlands. To look beyond our sense of helplessness and hopelessness, shame and failure. To see what really matters.

Too often it escapes our notice that the greatest sermon ever preached took place not in a brightly lit, ornately decorated, crowded cathedral, but in a plain farm field of a poor country beneath a dark sky in front of a few ordinary shepherds. Both the Good News and the best gift arrived at night. Jesus was born into a world much like our own. People were wrapped up in their own agendas, registering for the census, finding lodging, feeding donkeys, and tending sheep. They were also divorcing their wives and burying their dead. There was discrimination, high taxes, and political upheaval.

Our Savior never lead a sheltered life. As far as we know, he never hung a Christmas stocking or unwrapped a toy. Outside of traveling to Egypt as an infant, Jesus never journeyed more than a hundred miles from his birthplace. He didn't party with the elite, but chose to dine with commoners. He died at thirty-three, without decorating a Christmas tree or sending a card. What Jesus did do and still does is love people. He spoke with a divorcee, allowed a prostitute to wash his feet, and praised a poor widow who gave all she had.

Into our own dark December comes this undeserved and unbelievable love gift from the Father. You and I are accepted just as we are—moody or merry; rich or poor; married, widowed, or divorced. Judy in Ontario, Canada, puts it this way: "God's gift of salvation was given to us *before* we were divorced, widowed, wounded, abandoned, rejected, or homeless. This gift comes with an eternal, unchanging, non-negotiable, non-refundable guarantee."

As I read the closing words in her e-mail—*Emmanuel, God is with us*—I realized Judy lives moment to moment with this certainty. After serving beside her husband as a missionary in Africa for thirteen years, she is now a single working mom. Her husband of seventeen years claimed he had made a mistake marrying her and that he should not have to pay for that mistake for the rest of his life. Their divorce became final on December twenty-first. At Christmas, Judy struggles along with the rest of us over what to do with that box of ornaments from the past. But she knows what really matters—*Emmanuel*. She discovered that not even an unwanted divorce can separate her from God's love.

PRAYER PAUSE: *Father, thank you for seeing me as a whole, wonderful woman, who is full of promise and potential, and for gifting me with an ability to bless the world as I live out the truth of what I have been through. Your love overwhelms me.*

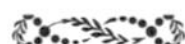

Love is a fruit in season at all times,
and within the reach of every hand.

MOTHER TERESA

42. *God, thanks for what was and what is yet to be.*

Be at rest once more, O my soul, for the Lord has been good to you.

PSALM 116:7 NIV

Be cautious and alert for snags [standing dead trees]. . . . They may fall without warning," read the brochure that I had picked up at the park entrance during a vacation.

As Richard and I drove the highway that snakes past lakes and sweeping vistas of the Grand Tetons and high plateaus crossing the Continental Divide, I saw snags wherever we went—along roadways and trails, in campsites and picnic areas. When we brushed passed them during a walk in the woods, they grabbed our socks and pulled our sweaters. I thought back to televised images of the firestorm that roared through the park in 1988. In its wake, thousands of snags now stand as reminders of that fiery conflagration, of a changed landscape and its lost wildlife.

In our lives, we also encounter reminders of the loss that changed us forever. Snags are everywhere—on the radio, in stores and restaurants, during holidays and family gatherings. Unannounced, they fall into our life and find our weak spot. A particular date on the calendar catches you unaware. Like a thorn, it pricks your heart. A song yanks your thoughts back to the past. A distinctive aroma replays a bittersweet event. An invitation to a celebration arrives, and your mind latches on to a memory . . . a time and place . . . and that person who is gone.

The biggest challenge with snags is not that they can unravel us, but that they will entangle us. They bore into that part of us that wants to extend the arc of mourning, indulge it, and will it to remain. Snags grip onto those doubts welling up on the crest of sleep. They claw at our fragile emotions and won't let us surface from the pain. Once they hook us, they take from us our will to live in the present and our hope to believe in a future. In the course of the journey, some of us get lost in the past. Our tears blind us to the possibility of young hopes sprouting through the ashes.

Looking back to that summer day when I stood beside those leafless, lifeless snags and saw only bare bark, charred chunks, and scorched skeletons, I realize God saw substance where I couldn't. Not only does God see seedlings spouting in the ashes of a blackened forest floor, but He sees our new beginnings, too. His tri-focal vision sees where we have been, where we are now, and where we are headed. He has not forgotten that once-lush forest of lodgepole pines—nor the person you and I were before our loss. He feels the whipping flames and rippling heat of the firestorm—and the suffering we undergo. When all we see are snags, God sees the women we were created to be and the growth still to come.

In fact, your presence here this moment is proof that God is still working in your life. Is there a better reason to give thanks?

PRAYER PAUSE: *Lord, some days all I see are snags, reminding me of what I've lost. When they come at me and grip my heart, I'm not sure I'll ever be able to pull loose. Thank you for keeping Your eyes on me in these unavoidable moments. In this season of doubt, I'm burrowing my faith deep into You.*[32]

What I spent, I lost. What I possessed is left to others.
What I gave away remains with me.

ANONYMOUS

My Mini Journal of Hope and Gratitude

. . . Through the dark valley of death . . . you are close beside me. PSALM 23:4

DATE	MY HARDEST DAYS	MY MOST PRECIOUS MEMORIES

Be like the bird that,
pausing on her flight awhile
on boughs too slight,
feels them give way beneath her,
and yet sings,
knowing that she hath wings.
VICTOR HUGO

My thanksgiving starts the instant I hear my relatives shift from park into reverse.

FROM CRABBY ROAD BY J. WAGNER

Daring Moments

When I Face My Fears

[Wo]man, like a bridge, was designed to carry the load of the moment, not the combined weight of a year all at once.

WILLIAM WARD

43. *Where's that knight on a white horse?*

I will strengthen and help you;
I will uphold you with my righteous right hand. . . .
For I am the Lord, your God, who takes hold of your right hand
and says to you, "Do not fear; I will help you."

ISAIAH 41: 10, 13 NIV

The longer we live, the more experience we have with losing. But that doesn't mean we get better at it. There are times we long for rescue.

Perhaps right now you are going through a divorce and are facing the loss of the familiar props upon which you built a life—your home, possessions, and social circle. Maybe you depended upon these props for your security. Or a loved one died and you are now forced to relinquish the roles you once played as somebody's wife, or mother, or daughter. These roles and accompanying relationships were your identity; they gave your life meaning and defined how you lived. Now you are wondering, *Where do I belong with no tangible history to back me up and nothing left to hold on to?*

When the props are knocked out from under us, the prospect of regrouping can seem terrifying. Our eyes open to the fact that life is not as we once thought and yet we must live it out. "I never expected life to be so messy," says Dr. Linda Snyderman, surgeon and medical correspondent for ABC News.[33]

Is it any wonder we long for rescue? A knight on a white horse to whisk us out of this mishmash. Ten quick ways to wipe up a bleeding heart. A miracle cure. Unfortunately, only two people were ever rescued out of this life—Elijah and Enoch. They escaped death. But Cathy Hainer didn't, despite her will to live. Her life, like ours, was full of plans and expectations. At thirty-six, she was a travel and feature reporter for *USA Today*. She expected to marry her fiancé, have his children, and grow old with him. But that was before cancer messed up her plans.

For two years, this gifted journalist chronicled for the nation's largest newspaper her battle with the same disease that took her mother's life. As I followed Cathy's story, I marveled at her fierce determination to live and her resolve to face the inevitable. Her words spoke with candor about every woman's fear. In her final installment, written before she died in December of 1999 of stage IV metastatic breast cancer, Cathy spoke of being imprisoned in her own body as she gradually lost her ability to do things. She described death as heartburn and revealed her conflict over deciding against more chemotherapy, all the while wondering how much effort a dying woman should make to rejoin life—*does she buy a new nightgown, floss teeth, pay bills, renew her driver's license?*

"I have to accept the fact that after months of outwitting death, it is now undeniably in my life. . . .No magic wizard at the end of my journey, no heart or lungs or magic balloon to give me a ride back to Kansas [as in the Wizard of Oz]," Cathy writes. "I have moments when the fear makes me sit up in bed at night and weep like a three-year-old. I've become afraid of the long, lonely nights. Yet at other times, I feel at peace, knowing I'm in the right place, secure in my beliefs about an afterlife."[34]

In the end, with the props knocked out from under her, Cathy Hainer seized what matters. She exchanged her frilly lingerie for the cotton comfort of hospital gowns. She gave up the head scarves that once covered her baldness and vanity. She let go of her long-range plans and treasured instead the lucid moments when she could visit pain free with friends and family before the drugs knocked her out. When the final curtain fell, she bravely took her bow. There was no Cinderella rescue or rewriting of her life's script. In the end, Cathy Hainer found security and resolution in her faith.

Both her fight to live and her struggle to die show us how loss strips us of nonessentials and points the way to our need for God who is our only deliverer.[35]

PRAYER PAUSE: *Lord, help me die to the false expectation that my security depends on perfect health and a perfect life. Teach me that I need resolve more than rescue. Wherever life takes me and for however long I'm here, I want to trust in You alone.*

If we could sell our experiences for what they cost us, we'd be millionaires.

ABIGAIL VAN BUREN

44. Examining my expectations

And He shall be the stability of your times.

ISAIAH 33:6 NASB

I love the paintings of Thomas Kinkade—his charming scenes of cottages nestled next to rose-covered arbors, of country churches tucked beside meandering streams, of lights in every window, and of idyllic gardens basking in a warm glow. I think what captures me is the image of an ideal world. In this dreamscape, my every wish is fulfilled. It is a place of well-being where I feel safe and secure, and where loss can't knock on the door.

We are all looking for this spot of tranquility, this idyllic abode. When life goes as we expect, well-being comes easy. So does faith. Most of us grew up expecting that if we are fair in our dealings, we'll be fairly treated. If we eat right and stop at red lights, we'll live a long, healthy life. If we work hard and save our money, we'll be financially secure. If we put others first and stay true to our commitments, we'll be happy and have happy relationships. Some of us were taught that if we trust God, our faith will keep us safe. If we believe hard enough and pray long enough, God will remove our problems. And, if we *have enough faith*, God will reconcile our relationships and heal our bodies.

It only takes one pedophile or overheated electrical circuit to debunk those happy misconceptions. Loss robs us of our illusions. Overnight, we wake up to the realization that a thief just broke into our cozy life and ran off with our sense of well-being. No longer do we live within a warm, glowing picture.

When your expectations about life and love are shattered, you get over building castles in the air. You discover there is no such place as an idyllic abode. You catch sight of how loss is moving you past your personal standards to what God expects of you. You start seeing how your expectations got in the way of reality, leading to disappointment. You begin to notice how the unrealistic and the unrealized distract you from what really matters. You see how much of your disappointment is because life, God, or somebody else failed to fulfill or live up to your expectations.

It has taken years, but I'm finally getting the picture. I expected more than this life could ever deliver. In the cold glare of reality, I now realize that life in this fallen world is not and has never been fair. It will never be a warm-fuzzy painting. *Life is what it is.*

Loss has also brought me to this rude awakening. *When I use my expectations to mentally paint a life free of disappointment and suffering, I am playing God.* I play God by creating a world that doesn't exist. I also play God when I fight over who is in control and refuse to live in the reality of what I know is true—the reality in which loss happens and people get hurt. The longer we live in the fantasy world we have painted for ourselves, the more real moments we will squander. To fully live, you and I must risk loss. That doesn't mean sanctioning what happens to us, but it does mean we let life be what it is and we trust God to be God.

PRAYER PAUSE: *Lord, nothing in this life is quite as I thought, and it scares me. I need You to be my point of reference about what is and is not true. Whatever it takes, illustrate Your image on the canvas of my life. Instead of living with a sense of entitlement, I want to live with a sense of eternity with my expectations firmly grounded in You.*

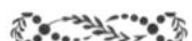

When your expectations for life are reduced to zero,
then everything becomes more meaningful.

DR. STEPHEN HAWKING, REFLECTING ON HIS TERMINAL ILLNESS

45. Daring to resuscitate dreams

Be strong and courageous. Do not be terrified; do not be discouraged, for the Lord your God will be with you wherever you go.

JOSHUA 1:9 NIV

Sometimes we just have to do it. To survive, we have to seize life. We have to step over the grave of that marriage that died in divorce. We have to toss out the wilted roses from the funeral of our loved one. We have to reconcile ourselves to living without the health we want, the happiness we deserve, or the people we need. We have to bury what isn't to make room for what is, so we aren't trapped in unlived lives.

Maybe you have always dreamed of completing your education or of adopting a child. Perhaps you have thought about changing careers and said (as I did), "Someday I'm going to write." Well, you can do it. You *alone* can do it. *Alone* means *all one* or *wholly one*. God has already given you *all* you need (2 Peter 1:3). It really is wholly up to you. You don't need another person or another thing to breathe life into your dream.

Dreams come in all shapes and sizes—from aspirations and reveries to images and thoughts passing through the mind during sleep. Do you know that the Bible is full of dreamers? During a dream, Solomon received a divine vision where God appeared and asked him what he wished for. God was pleased with Solomon's response and gave him a wise and discerning heart (1 Kings 3:5-15). Jacob had a dream of seeing God standing above a ladder of angels ascending to heaven. God promised Jacob the land on which he slept (Genesis 28:10-22). At first, Joseph's dreams landed him in a pit. But after interpreting Pharaoh's dreams, he was elevated to Egypt's second in command (Genesis 37; 41). Another Joseph dreamed of an angel. He received startling answers as to why his fiancé, Mary, was pregnant (Matthew 1:19-24).

Someone once said that dreams are the stuff of life. I have friends who say when life gets too stuffed with obligations, they dream of heaven. All of us have dreams—those aspirations we imagine might be possible and the thoughts we visualize. Our Creator uses these dreams to reveal His will, to keep us from evil, and to encourage and instruct us about life.[36] Some of us have compromised our dream for other people's values because *we didn't fit in* or *it just wasn't done*. Others of us gave up our dream. We buried it out of fear. As a result, we left behind an important piece of ourselves. That dream may have been the most important thing God gifted us to do in the world.

Catherine Marshall was a dreamer. She was only twenty-three when she moved with her husband, Peter, to Washington, D.C. He became pastor of the New York Avenue Presbyterian Church and later served as U.S. Chaplain. At the peak of their ministry, she was diagnosed with tuberculosis. Doctors claimed she would recover in just a few months, but two years later she was still struggling with the disease. Catherine also battled depression. Out of those experiences she wrote:

Once I had such big dreams, so much anticipation of the future.
Now no shimmering horizon beckons me . . .
You have told us that without vision, we men perish.
So, Father in heaven, knowing that I can ask in confidence
for what is Your expressed will to give me,
I ask You to deposit in my mind and heart that particular dream,
the special vision You have for my life.[37]

After her husband's sudden death, Catherine Marshall went on to become an internationally renowned writer and speaker. She frequently talked about the years of isolation in her bedroom as the place where God taught her to depend on Him alone and where she dared to believe she could dream again.

You, too, can find the courage to revive your dream. Something deep inside you is telling you that you just have to do it. And you *will* dare to do it, because the life within you is becoming more stubborn than death.

PRAYER PAUSE: *Father, when the time is right, help me resuscitate the dreams You gave me long ago. I don't want fear to shrink my world or steal my dreams.*

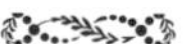

Dreams are renewable.
No matter what our age or condition,
there are still untapped possibilities within us
and new beauty waiting to be born.

DR. DALE TURNER

46. Rediscovering my worth

I waited patiently for the Lord to help me,
and he turned to me and heard my cry.
He lifted me out of the pit of despair, . . . He set my feet on solid ground
and steadied me as I walked along.

PSALM 40:1-2

Underneath the months of grief, you are discovering a woman whose life is still worthwhile. As a living legacy of what you have been through, you realize you are wiser and more valuable than you think. You are accepted and loved just as you are. You belong to something much larger than yourself.

Acceptance. Love. Belonging. Worth. That's the sense I get when I snuggle under my grandmother's quilt. Beneath its colorful patchwork, I feel safe and warm. (No wonder they call them comforters!) Under the quilt, I reminisce about my grandmother, knowing that she was thinking of me as she pieced together the scraps and swatches of worn-out clothing. Every pierce of the needle and each snip of the thread bears witness to the time and energy she invested in this quilt. My grandmother created this one-of-a-kind masterpiece because she thought I was worth it. That is what God is doing for us.

We are His fancywork. Out of the remnants in our lives, God is creating something beautiful and unique. He uses each scar and tear, entwining our weakness with His strength to make whole cloth. He stitches up our doubts and fears and re-embroiders our tattered hope and faded joy. Each experience we go through bears witness to God's investment in us. Nothing is wasted. As He binds up our brokenness, God is thinking about us. God does all this and more because we are worth it. Yet so many of us don't feel deserving.

We have found out the hard way that if other people don't approve of our performance or appearance, they might abandon us. Some people leave us physically. Others leave us with a loud message that we are not enough. We are not good enough or pretty enough. We did not do enough, or what we did do was less than the best. Before long, we're telling ourselves, *I'm no good. I can't do anything right.*

Counselor and teacher Bob George illustrates this point with the story of a boy who draws a picture with crayons for his mother. She rants and raves about how good the drawing is and what talent her son has. As a result, the boy figures his mother will like him even more if he draws a bigger picture. He scampers to his bedroom and finds a blank wall—and, well, we all know what happens next. "One minute, you're a genius. The next minute, you're stupid," says Bob George.[38]

Major loss can also smother the worth right out of us. We are left thinking, *I'm no use to anybody now. I'm not important to the world. Nobody loves me.* We gaze into the mirror, bothered because we're losing our looks. Or we tie our identity to our body size and image, to our job or achievements, the clothes we wear, the cars we drive, or the people we know. When life becomes a contest, our worth is up for grabs. There is always somebody else prettier, younger, richer, or better.

We forget that there is more to life than fitting an image or winning a contest. There's value to having survived a lifetime of experience with soul and sanity intact. There is merit in adapting to unexpected change and living with catastrophic loss. Real worth isn't measured by our successes or failures. We aren't worth more if our children turn out well but less if they turn out badly.

Even loss cannot diminish us, but it can remake us, by growing us up and enlarging our hearts. Some of us are being fashioned into comforters; we spread the compassion and security that God is lavishly bestowing on us by wrapping others with His love when they hurt (II Corinthians 1:3-4).

PRAYER PAUSE: *Lord Jesus, sometimes I forget how very important I am to You. Help me remember that I am uniquely created, divinely gifted, and so loved that if I were the only person on earth You would still sacrifice Your life for me. Keep reminding me that the deepest source of my identity is in You. I am more than enough simply because I belong to You.*

How silent the woods would be if only the best birds sang.

ANONYMOUS

47. Could I love and trust again?

But in my distress I cried out to the Lord; yes, I prayed to my God for help.
He heard me from his sanctuary; my cry reached his ears.

PSALM 18:6

At one time or another, we all lose trust. People lose trust in us. We lose trust in others and in ourselves. We also lose trust in God. Rebuilding trust is hard work.

We are taught to trust. Trust is a crucial element of faith—faith in others, ourselves, and God. Trust is the best gift one spouse gives the other and is critical in any other relationship. That is why relationships disintegrate when someone violates our trust. We lose faith, second-guess our judgment, and become afraid to love and trust anyone else ever again.

Following a catastrophic loss, we can lose trust in life, in everyone and everything around us, because it appears that all the pain and evil in the world has targeted us and won. Our sacred space has been invaded. We feel violated.

Violations of any kind alienate us, but especially if it involves a personal betrayal. Perhaps someone you loved betrayed your trust. They penetrated your reality and forced theirs upon you, telling you what you saw, thought, heard, and felt was false. Because you wanted to believe them, you suspended your disbelief and trusted them—again and again. Like an invisible rape, their lies assaulted your mind and spirit. But instead of losing your virginity, you lost your innocence. Now you wonder if they ever told you the truth. If the betrayer was someone before whom you bared body or soul in marriage, you question what you have been taught about loving and trusting—and you may even distrust God, because He did not keep you safe.

Healing this kind of wound does not happen overnight. But trust can be relearned, changing you for the better. Lina in California, survivor of an emotionally abusive marriage, says, "What we perceive, or what the other person is telling us, is not always the truth. I have learned to be much more cautious in trusting, to use the wisdom God has blessed me with, and to never again think I'm so powerful that I can change someone's nature."

Like Lina, we cannot change the fact that we live in a world of deception, but we can become more discerning about whom to trust and how much. We cannot stop people from lying, but we can recognize how they distort our reality and divert our search for truth. But to get there, we must do what the deceiver cannot—come back into wholeness in the light of truth.

Before my divorce, I missed the truth of I Corinthians 13:7. Thinking I was "being biblical," I let myself trust an untrustworthy man. But the Bible does not tell us to trust others. It emphasizes being trustworthy, warns us about putting our trust in others (Psalm 146:3), and says that only God can be counted on (Jeremiah 17:5, 7; Proverbs 29:25). Because God is trustworthy, we are able to entrust ourselves to Him. Through Him, you and I can extend love and trust to others.

As you trust God and live out the principles you know to be true, you rebuild trust in yourself. Instead of being humiliated over past encounters with deception, you let them teach you that not every story rings true and that not everyone is guided by your ethical, moral, and spiritual values. Now you watch people's footsteps—where they are heading and not just what they are saying. You notice the message beneath their words. When you sense the emotional commotion that liars use to conceal truth, you find the courage to confront them. You hold them responsible to earn your trust.

In time, you begin to trust that you can handle whatever life throws at you and you no longer mistrust your own judgment. No matter what other people say or do, you make God's standard your own and you hold it up—especially in wolf country, where innocent doves need the shrewdness of snakes (Matthew 10:16).

PRAYER PAUSE: *Lord, sometimes I'm not sure if I will ever be able to love or trust again. My innocence is shattered and I've lost confidence. Give me a wise heart and a discerning mind. For now, it's enough to entrust myself to You.*

To be trusted is a greater compliment than to be loved.

GEORGE MACDONALD

48. Sending my anxiety on vacation

Worry weighs a person down. . . .

PROVERBS 12:25

You can't believe that dreaded uneasiness is back. But this time it is born of fear, not grief. Fear of the unknown. Fear of starting over. Fear that you won't make it. After all you have been through, you know you are stronger than you feel—until you get that anxious flutter when you need to function. You tell yourself it won't last, but you're finding it hard to tolerate uncertainty. You wonder what you'll lose next and how you'll cope.

If you are constantly concerned about *what might happen next*, fear and worry are fueling anxiety. And when anxiety pays a visit, it's time to send it packing. Anxiety is generalized fear. It can impair your life. Life doesn't stop making demands on you because you can't manage your fears. Psychologist Gary Emery, Ph.D., director of the Los Angeles Center for Cognitive Therapy, says, "The precursor to anxiety is uncertainty."[39] That's why anxiety is often triggered by a loss.

As women we are especially vulnerable. We are the world's caretakers, juggling home and work, along with the needs of our family. Our lives are compressed and stressed. In times of grief, we not only mourn our own losses, but try to help our children through their pain as well. Then, we worry over not being able to do more or that we didn't do enough. Some level of concern is necessary for our survival, but too much is as dangerous to our health as high blood pressure. We cannot anticipate and rehearse how to avoid everything that might go wrong. But a lot of us try—especially at night.

No wonder we think it is darkest before the dawn. As Seneca said, "Night brings our troubles to light, rather than banishing them." We can get so consumed with our fears that we take them to bed. We toss and turn, pondering our plight and watching the clock. Yet most of the things we imagine never come to pass.

When life spirals out of control, fear of the unknown is common. It's not that we don't have enough faith; it's because we are human. I am so glad that Jesus identified with our humanity. He hiked to the top of the Mount of Olives and openly spoke about our anxiety (Matthew 6:25-34). As a keen observer of Mary and Martha, Jesus knew that women have plenty to juggle; they don't need to factor in the weight of tomorrow. So He said, "Do not be anxious for tomorrow; for tomorrow will care for itself. Each day has enough trouble of its own" (Matthew 6:34 NASB).

The next time you are mentally replaying a situation and envisioning disaster, pause and focus on what is going right. Talk to yourself like a friend instead of a critic, and start separating facts from what *might happen*. If you fear another catastrophe, remember that you've been there before. You know the worst case scenario—you survived the pain. Give yourself permission *now* to quit stewing about a future that you cannot control, just as you gave yourself permission *then* to accept what could not be changed. Corrie ten Boom's advice still rings true: "Worry does not empty tomorrow of its sorrow; it empties today of its strength."

PRAYER PAUSE: *Lord, I'm tired of running scared. Help me accept what I can't control . . . and that the world won't end if I fail.*

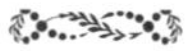

Our fears are more numerous than our dangers,
and we suffer much more in apprehension than in reality.

SENECA, 4 B.C.

49. Lord, stay with me through this fear.

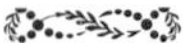

Keep me safe, O God, for I have come to you for refuge.

PSALM 16:1

We have all entertained it. We know its squeeze on our heart and its lump in our throat. We've tasted its dryness in our mouth and wiped its sweat from our brow. Fear is unsettling and demanding. It freeze-dries us in our tracks. What underlies fear is a loss of control.

Whatever you are going through, you know that fear is real—whether you experience it as a panic attack, a simple misgiving, a phobia, anxiety, or icy terror. Fear slithers under your insecurities and doubts to bully you into submission.

I once had a neighbor who lived with agoraphobia—the fear of open spaces. Elinor's life was limited to a ten-block area. She was afraid to drive and refused to ride in a car with anyone but her husband. If he deviated one street from her predetermined route to the market, she would panic. Elinor never set foot in her daughter's house or watched her granddaughter play in the high school band because she was shackled by fear. Until the day she died, it controlled everything she did.

According to Dr. Dean Ornish, clinical professor of medicine at the University of California–San Francisco, our hearts can shut down in fear, separating us from the love we need—especially from the fear that someone won't love us. "We literally starve, because we cut ourselves off from that larger life force," Ornish says. "Every time there is worry, or fear, there is stress; and I've always defined stress as that which is isolating. Anything that takes you out of the sense of connection stresses you."[40]

We were never meant to live with such fear. It restricts us from fully living. But whenever we encounter loss, we also run smack dab into our fears. Fear that we can't cope. Fear of the unknown. Fear we won't be able to trust again. Fear we will never feel whole again. Maybe that's why the Bible tells us that perfect love casts out fear (I John 4:18). God, who embodies perfect love, did not create us to be held captive by our fears. At the cross, He liberated us from our greatest fear—the fear of eternal death. Throughout Scripture, we are reminded to "take courage" and "fear not."

Right now, whatever fear is detaining you, you can be confident that God is with you,the way He was with the apostle Paul in that Macedonian jail (Acts 16:20-36). Although your situation may not be changing any time soon, God promises to give you peace of mind and heart as you stand your ground and stare down your fears. Christ said, "I am leaving you with a gift—peace of mind and heart. . . . So don't be troubled or afraid" (John 14:27).

A while back Donna Bechtel, who served beside her husband for seventeen years as a missionary to Hong Kong, spoke to our women's Bible study. She told the story of her mother, who was a pastor's wife in the 1940s. Minutes before her mother was scheduled to step on stage to sing a duet in an evening service, her pastor-husband pulled her aside and said, "I'm leaving you." Needless to say, this young mother of five, with one child under a month old, was frightened to death—until she glanced down at the song title. From that moment on, she claimed its words as God's promise to her.

Donna said her mother wiped away her tears, bravely walked into that sanctuary, and sang, "God Will take Care of You." In the years that followed, Donna grew up "watching God's people work" as they tended to the family's physical needs and graced them with compassion. "As I watched my mother live out what she believed, it built up my faith," Donna says.

God Will Take Care of You[41]
Be not dismay'd whate'er betide,
Beneath his wings of love abide,
Thro' days of toil when heart doth fail,
When dangers fierce your path assail,
No matter what may be the test,
Lean, weary one, upon his breast.
God will take care of you, Thro' ev'ry day, o'er all the way
He will take care of you, God will take care of you.

PRAYER PAUSE: *God, my fears are driving me to my knees. Yet I know I cannot speak of courage unless I experience fear. Only You can show me where to go from here.*

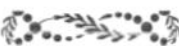

You gain strength, courage, and confidence
by every experience in which
you really stop to look fear in the face.

ELEANOR ROOSEVELT

My Mini Journal of Hope and Gratitude

For God hath not given us the spirit of fear,
but of power . . . love . . . a sound mind. 2 TIMOTHY 1:7 KJV

DATE	MY BIGGEST FEARS	MY HOPES AND DREAMS

Stay present. You will always have time to worry later on if you want to.

DAN MILLMAN

The Second Commandments

1. You shall not worry, for worry is the most unproductive of all human activities.
2. You shall not be fearful, for most of the things we fear never come to pass.
3. You shall not cross bridges before you come to them, for no one yet has succeeded in accomplishing this.
4. You shall face each problem as it comes. You can only handle one at a time anyway.
5. You shall not take problems to bed with you, for they make very poor bedfellows.
6. You shall not borrow other people's problems. They can better care for them than you can.
7. You shall not try to relive yesterday for good or ill; it is forever gone. Concentrate on what is happening in your life and be happy now.
8. You shall be a good listener, for only when you listen do you hear ideas different from your own. It is hard to learn something new when you are talking, and some people do know more than you do.
9. You shall not become "bogged down" by frustration, for ninety percent of it is rooted in self-pity and will only interfere with positive action.
10. You shall count your blessings, never overlooking the small ones, for a lot of small blessings add up to a big one.

—Author unknown[42]

Decisive Moments

That Fuel Change and Clarify My Perspective

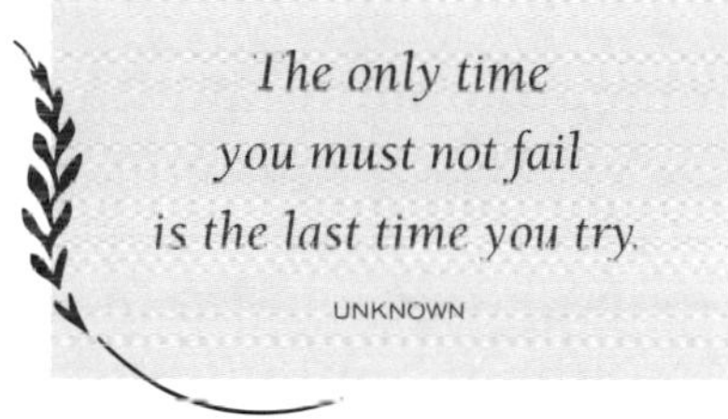

The only time
you must not fail
is the last time you try.
UNKNOWN

50. I didn't deserve this

O God, you have ground me down and devastated my family. . . .
My eyes are red with weeping; darkness covers my eyes.
Yet I am innocent, and my prayer is pure.

JOB 16:7, 16, 17

You don't want to dig too deep in Susan Howard's garden. It is where she buries her troubles and battles her anger. If anyone understands how Job dared to question God and why he cursed his life, Susan does. Two years ago she lost her eldest son. But that's only part of her story.

In the early years of her marriage to Rick, both of Susan's parents died, her brother-in-law was killed in a shooting accident, and she gave birth to two sons with cystic fibrosis. "This disease is progressive, long, and tiring," says Susan. "At both Morgan's and Loren's births, my husband and I agreed that the only way we could survive was to keep things as normal as possible."

Two years ago Susan was diagnosed with non-Hodgkin lymphoma, but she had to delay chemotherapy because of stress over her son's upcoming surgery. Morgan was scheduled for a living donor lung transplant—one lobe from a teacher, the other from his dad. After the procedure, the endotracheal tube came loose. Morgan went into cardiac arrest and had a stroke. He was neurologically damaged from oxygen deprivation to the brain.

With Rick also in the hospital as a donor-patient, Susan bore the load of breaking the news to him and Loren, and consulting with the physicians. For four weeks, she hobbled along the corridors with an elephant leg on her left side and enlarged lymph nodes in her groin—painful reminders of the growing lymphoma.

She lived in the waiting room, bathroom, and her car. Morgan never recovered. He was twenty-three years old when he died.

"I would give anything to hear him cough again," says Susan. "If you're the mother, it affects you differently. You carried this child inside you. I told God, 'I don't want to be here anymore. Take me instead.'" A year later Susan entered into chemotherapy, but her hoped-for spontaneous remission never came. She admits there were days when she raised her hands to the heavens and asked, "Is not enough *enough*?" Yet nothing compared to losing Morgan—not the death of her parents, not the cancer.

"I still have no desire to get up in the morning," she says. "I have trouble getting through the day and going to sleep at night, because I'm haunted by what they did to my baby." But regardless of how bad it gets—including Rick's recent diagnosis of type II diabetes and Loren's third back surgery—she is determined to find something good in each day.

"I never ever said *'I don't deserve this.'* Who is to say who deserves what? There's always somebody worse off than you are," says Susan. "Instead, I ask, 'What am I supposed to learn?' Then, I semi-raise my sword to this dragon of adversity in my life and say, 'I acknowledge you for what you are. Now I'm going out to the garden and dig a hole.' Each time I pull weeds, pick a flower, or trim trees, I try to look for something positive, even if I don't see it.'"

PRAYER PAUSE: *Lord, haven't I borne more than my share? Show me what I can't see. In the meantime, give me strength to crawl out of bed tomorrow and get through the day.*

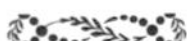

There are times . . . when things seem so bad that you've got to grab your fate by the shoulders and shake it.

ANONYMOUS

51. *Why do my friends lead such charmed lives?*

Enjoy what you have rather than desiring what you don't have. Just dreaming about nice things is meaningless; it is like chasing the wind. Everything has already been decided. It was known long ago what each person would be. So there's no use arguing with God about your destiny.

ECCLESIASTES 6:9-10

If you haven't said it, you've probably thought it—*Why me, and not them*? That is because when we are hurting, we feel singled out if others' lives appear easier than our own. In the midst of Job's calamities, he certainly voiced concern over the prosperity of the wicked (Job 21:7-17).

I admit, this is an area with which I often struggle. I remember when my daughter was in grade school, I detested magazine articles describing how to raise a well-behaved, high-achieving child—because Melanie did not fit the mold. She was hyperactive, with concentration and short-term-memory problems. She battled with reading, pronouncing one painful sentence after another, word by word, sound by sound. She chattered through church and bounced up and down in school. I tried everything from a private school to drug therapy and tutoring, but nothing helped. She felt like a failure, and so did I—especially when I looked at other parents and wondered, *Why do things work out for them?* As my exasperation grew, I grew angry at my situation and envious of others.

Maybe you're angry about a divorce. You lost not only a husband but also the loyalty of your children. You are no longer invited to social events, and major decisions are made without you. You know that your children are siding with their dad for fear that he might leave them the way he left you, but you can't help resenting the unfairness. You haven't shared your frustration with another soul because no one else has this problem. How you envy their supposed conflict-free lifestyle.

Resentment has to be one of our most volatile emotions, because it inflames us with envy and jealousy. Envy destroys friendships. Jealousy rips apart families. Both can fuel revenge. But the greatest danger is that these emotions can divert us from God's unique plan for our lives and leave us with a bitter taste that lingers a lifetime. We become meanspirited.

Someone once observed that hurting people will either act like a skunk that sprays everyone in sight or a turtle that withdraws into a shell. Resentment will consume us if we let it. As Dr. Charles Stanley says, "There is nothing worse than a life filled with adversity from which nothing *good* ever comes."[43]

What helps me, as I struggle with this, is realizing that drawing comparisons is a typical grief response. When we are hurting, we will be tempted to see others' lives as more charmed than our own. We fan resentment into existence because it feeds our hurts. But we don't have to stay that way. Life's too short to waste holding a grudge. We have things to do and people to bless. Besides, being envious and critical of others is not worth the risk of missing God's one-of-a-kind plan for *our* life.

PRAYER PAUSE: *Lord, I get so upset when I look around at other people—their happy families and their together marriages. I want what they have. Help me to stop comparing myself with others and to realize that I am still in process.*

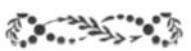

If you're green with envy, you're ripe for trouble.

ANONYMOUS

52. How anger keeps me stuck

Guide my steps by your word, so I will not be overcome by any evil.

PSALM 119:133

Anger is often the impetus of change. It is an emotional wish for things to be different. In the middle of a life-altering disease or a life-changing loss, anger will assert itself and demand our attention.

Anger can be healthy, if it fuels re-engagement with life. It can become the main thrust of our will to live. It energizes the fight-for-your-life response that wants to know: *What's next? And where do I go from here?*

But anger also can be unhealthy, if we expend too much energy stuffing it or plotting revenge. Instead of the will to live, anger can fuel the desire to die. That's why anger is a powerful force to be reckoned with.

Because anger is part of the debris of loss, first, we must acknowledge its presence and our need to deal with it. Next, we must clear its blockage from our heart, as we would lavage dirt from a wound. If we don't, anger festers into rage and infects our spirit with bitterness. "You shove it down and don't realize you're doing it," says Phoebe Steiger. "After my husband died, I had problems sleeping, and now I believe it was because I stuffed my anger."

Anger is not nearly as frightening if we can find a positive way to harness it. One way is by talking to someone. When you speak of your anger aloud, you bring it out in the open. Another way is dialoguing with yourself in a journal. Just as David expressed in Psalm 109, written words are a way of screaming out your anger to God. However you choose to bear witness to the experience that made you angry and to express how you truly feel, you are acknowledging anger's existence and releasing its power over you.

Sometimes we are angry over what is left undone, and we don't even realize it. Let's say you arrived too late at the deathbed, and there wasn't the luxury to say a final goodbye. Maybe you never found the words to bring closure to a marriage that died. Or when someone close to you suddenly passed away, you discovered they never told you their condition was terminal because they wanted to spare you the worry. Anger has a way of reminding us of these unresolved issues, of the words we left unsaid, and of the words of others that we never heard. It brings to mind the grieving we have yet to do.

In the three years since Phoebe's husband died, she has struggled with her anger. She has good reason to be angry. During a routine checkup, a doctor thought he felt something on Brad's prostate and referred him to a urologist for a biopsy. Brad and Phoebe assumed everything was fine, because they never heard otherwise. It wasn't until he developed a facial rash and lost his balance that they learned he had cancer. He was finally diagnosed with stage 4 prostate cancer; but by this time, it had metastasized from his prostate to his lungs and brain. On his sixtieth birthday, surgeons removed a brain tumor. The family rejoiced after learning it was benign; but a week later, doctors admitted they had made a mistake. The tumor was malignant.

Because Brad wanted a second opinion, Phoebe says she picked up his records at the hospital, and out of curiosity pulled off to the side of the road to read them. "I found two different places in the stack of records in his file at the hospital where the doctor had written 'suspicious of malignancy,'" she says. "I was stunned. We both were angry. But I stuffed it deep, trying to get through each day, because Brad wasn't himself at that point. Whether the cancer would have been discovered a year earlier, we'll never know."

Phoebe describes the final months of Brad's life as a feeling of having already lost him. They no longer communicated as two adults. Her husband of forty-one years was now forgetful. He put on wool shirts in the summer and wore three pairs of underwear. Phoebe pleaded with God. "I could not imagine Brad not being in my bed at night, so I told God, 'Even though Brad is like this, I would like him to stay,'" says Phoebe.

Phoebe admits to moments when she still questions why, especially when she sees couples in their fifties and sixties walking in the park or grandfathers pushing grandchildren in the swings. "I'm in a group nobody wants to join," she says, "But I try to look at what happened as God's way of allowing me to lose my husband gradually." Now that Phoebe is able to verbalize her anger over having to make decisions alone and at herself for not catching on right away to Brad's deteriorating health, she says that she can sleep.

Along with Phoebe, you and I can release anger's stranglehold on our lives by bringing it out in the open. Life is too short to keep stuffing it.

PRAYER PAUSE: *God, help me release anger's stranglehold. I cannot afford to stay stuck.*

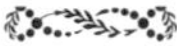

For ever minute you remain angry,
you give up sixty seconds of peace of mind.

RALPH WALDO EMERSON

53. Bitter is not a place I want to be

Then I realized how bitter I had become,
how pained I had been by all I had seen. . . .
I must have seemed like a senseless animal to you.
Yet I still belong to you; you are holding my right hand.

PSALM 73:21-23

As Christians, we believe that this life is the only one we get to live. In the Bible we read that God's original intention in Eden was perfection: No sin, no pain, no unjust gain. No conflict or loss. No death or divorce. Lots of freedom with only one restriction. God wanted to spare us the experience of evil.

But in a fallen world, it doesn't quite work that way. No wonder we are outraged at evil and angry at loss. We were never intended to live with the trauma of betrayal, rejection, abandonment, or the death of a loved one. In the tenth chapter of Job, his disgust with life mirrors our own. We can understand how he could say, "I will speak in the bitterness of my soul" (Job 10:1).

"In a way, the Garden is always with us," says John Townsend, cofounder and codirector of Cloud-Townsend Clinic and Communications in Newport Beach, California. "Our memories of good moments, and our wishes for ourselves and others to be better, keep the image of the ideal in our hearts. At times this encourages us. Sometimes it torments us. We think, *I shouldn't have made that error—I knew better. Why did I let it happen again?*"

If you were a good-hearted woman in love with a two-timing man, you are well acquainted with the haunting *shoulds* and *shouldn'ts* of which Townsend speaks. You also know how a "root of bitterness" seizes the slightest opening, then slithers into your spirit like a snake. And grows. Bitter isn't just an emotion you can feel, but what you can become. One who seethes with revenge and scoffs at life. Bitterness kills our spirit and eventually destroys our soul. This is what Gerald Sittser calls "the second death." "The first kind of death happens *to* us [loss of spouse, children, parents, health, job, marriage, childhood]; the second kind of death happens *in* us," he says. "It is a death we bring upon ourselves if we refuse to be transformed by the first death."[44]

Unresolved anger works in our hearts like stalagmites and stalactites in a cave. Slowly, it builds up, one drop at a time, until it accumulates and becomes something substantial. It reminds me of the hard water from our well. Although we have dirt filters, a water softener, and a reverse osmosis system that removes most of the minerals, we can't get rid of them all. I have to keep buffing the hard water spots off the faucet handles and the shower tiles or else the deposits will build up.

Over time unresolved anger develops into a bitter attitude and becomes a state of mind. Not only does it harden our hearts but it can leave us with steely-squinty eyes, thin pressed-together lips, and unwanted frown lines around our mouth. I don't think bitter is a place any of us want to be.

PRAYER PAUSE: *Father, thanks for accepting me—anger and all. Help me break down the barriers in my heart, mind, and soul. I want to make peace with this flawed world, with others' frail natures, and with my own flaws and frailness. Enable me to work through my anger early, before it hardens my heart.*

Bitterness is a lack of forgiveness multiplied many times over.

DR. CHARLES STANLEY

54. Realizing the past is no longer an option

But forget all that—it is nothing compared to what I am going to do.
For I am about to do a brand-new thing. See, I have already begun!
Do you not see it? I will make a pathway through
the wilderness for my people to come home.
I will create rivers for them in the desert!

ISAIAH 43:18-19

There are times when we stand at the threshold of a decision that will determine the direction of the rest of our lives. How we decide to deal with our anger at loss is one of them. Unfortunately, we may not always see the subtle way loss anchors us to the past—or how our anger over the *what ifs* and *might have beens* keeps us attached.

The reason many of us find it hard to pry our fingers off the past is because we know how quickly the people we love, the possessions we treasure, and the places in which we find shelter can be ripped from our arms. When we lose the one person we thought would love us for a lifetime or the home we spent years decorating, we discover that we can be severed from our moorings. When we must relinquish traditions because they are too painful to repeat and no longer have meaning, we chafe at being cut adrift. We watch in disbelief as strangers at our garage sale snatch up the possessions we spent years accumulating. We stare in horror as the hem of our wedding dress flaps out of the cardboard box being carted off to charity.

Our heart is torn, and we are angry at our situation. Yet we tremble at the thought of the unknown. We don't know if we have it in us to face it. Like battered women who remain in abusive relationships, we think that what we have is better than nothing at all. That is how anger over our losses keeps us stuck.

I love the greeting card illustration by artist Lisi Martin that shows a young girl standing at an intersection looking up at a road sign. The sign reads, "Believe in yourself." One way points to The Past. The other way points to The Future. The girl is concentrating on the arrow directing her toward the future. With a bouquet of flowers in her hand, a satchel on her shoulder, and a carpetbag at her feet, she stands the way we do at the threshold of a decision.

I remember standing at just such an intersection during my divorce. When I looked back at The Past, it seemed so inviting. I was familiar with its nooks and crannies, its twists and turns—and, unfortunately, its crazymaking. I had lived there and it was all I knew. The Future was frightening. The road heading that direction was unknown. As I teetered on the threshold of a decision, what helped me most was the startling realization that The Past was no longer an option. I could not go back, even if I wanted to.

Deb, who lives in New Hampshire, recently wrote to me about an intersection in her own life. She had been married for thirty years when her husband left. He divorced her because he was in love with his "Christian" secretary. After the divorce, she decided not to remarry but to pray that he would come back to her. For seven years, Deb put her life on hold. When her ex-husband remarried last year, she was devastated. She says it was like the divorce had happened all over again. After months of working through her anger, Deb came to a decision and this is what she wrote:

"On this day I have finally made the decision that I will not live another day, minute, or second with the guilt that I could have done more to make my marriage work. Thank you for your wonderful book [*When He Leaves*]. It is my story. I realized that my husband had been unfaithful to me for twenty-seven out of the thirty years we were married. Lies were thrown at me, so I was convinced that I 'had a problem.' Now I am excited about my life and I know that the Lord is opening up new challenges for me."

Loss is not something that any of us invites into our lives, but somehow it finds us. We are forced to make decisions we would never be asked to make otherwise. As you stand at the threshold of a decision that will determine the direction of the rest of your life, remember you are not alone. Many women have stood in your shoes. Some of us will choose The Future right away. The rest of us are like Deb; we take awhile. Sure, it's scary. Yes, the terrain is unknown. But it's the right road. Someday, you'll glance back and wonder why you ever hesitated at the intersection in the first place.

PRAYER PAUSE: *Heavenly Father, it's so difficult to leave the past behind when I can't even see a future and I don't have a clue what it holds. I'm willing to try, if You go with me—one step at a time, one day at a time.*

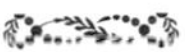

You cannot step twice into the same river,
for other waters are continually flowing on.

HERACLITUS

55. Willing myself to forgive so I may heal

I have the desire to do what is good,
but I cannot carry it out. . . . Who will rescue me . . . ?
Thanks be to God—through Jesus Christ, our Lord!

ROMANS 7:18, 24, 25 NIV

Forgiveness is critical if we want to move forward with our lives. It is the bridge from death to life. It spans the distance between the wounds and wrongs of a past that we cannot change, and a future we cannot anticipate. Forgiveness is the most Godlike act we will ever attempt on earth, because it is the ultimate act of love. Based on the principle that God has already forgiven us, we forgive others instead of seeking revenge because we recognize that we, too, owe a debt that we cannot repay.

Forgiveness means that we give up our right to be repaid or get even. It is a positive response to someone else's negative behavior. However, reconciling with the past does not mean we forget what happened. "Actually forgiveness is a decision one makes because one remembers," says John Splinter.[45] Forgiveness begins with our *willingness to be willing* to forgive and ends with our wishing another well. It is not a feeling, but an act of the will. It is not a one-time option, but an ongoing choice. When we forgive, it does not mean we must take that person back or allow him to "do it to us one more time." Forgiveness includes identifying evil, harm, and injustice for what they are—not tolerating them.

According to Lewis Smedes, former professor of theology and philosophy of religion at Fuller Theological Seminary, anger over what someone does to us is not an indication we have not forgiven, but means we get mad when people do bad things to us. "The enemy of forgiving is hate, not anger," Smedes says.[46]

During a tour of China, I met two women who have reason to hate—Mitsuko, a San Francisco State University professor, and Nancy, an English-speaking tour guide in Chongquing. Both women grew up on opposite sides of World War II. Mitsuko was in sixth grade when an American bombing raid destroyed her parents' home in Tokyo. "Every night the bombs fell like rain," she says. As for Nancy, when the Japanese bombed Shanghai, her grandparents were killed. Neither harbors hate but say they recognize there were two sides to the story, revealing a bigger picture.

For us to cross over from our personal view of life's inequities to the opposite side of the picture, we must forgive. From there we can see our own evil while discovering the humanity of those who wronged us, whether he is the drunk driver who killed our child, or that spouse who abandoned us.

How can we say, "The one who hurt me does not deserve forgiveness"? We do not deserve it either. Our hateful thoughts and the hateful acts others commit against us are both sin. God hates sin, not the sinner. He sent Jesus to die for sin and to save sinners. No sin is beyond His love. "Forgiveness is built on mercy and grace," says Dr. Norman Geisler. "Mercy is [God] not giving us what we did deserve; grace is [God] giving us what we didn't deserve."[47] Forgiveness is the one bridge you and I don't want to burn. It provides passage to where God wants us to be.

PRAYER PAUSE: *Lord, make me willing to be willing to forgive.*

Everyone says forgiveness is a wonderful idea
until they have someone to forgive.

C. S. LEWIS

56. *Father, help me learn to let go.*

The eternal God is your refuge, and underneath are the everlasting arms.

DEUTERONOMY 33:27 NIV

Women are life's keepers. Letting go is against our nature. Just look at our closets. We like to hold on. Mull over our memories. Keep traditions alive. Treasure our trinkets. Not only do we clutch people and possessions, but we also anchor ourselves to places. We don't want to pull up stakes. It is frightening to start over. Move to a different neighborhood. Live in an unfamiliar setting. Attend a new church. Get acquainted with strangers.

We are afraid of what lies beyond our comfort zone. It seems easier to stay with what we know. We think if we hold on, nothing will change. But it does. Life's losses force us to see that nothing remains as it once was. Change forces us to choose between staying stuck or stepping forward, between giving up or letting go.

Letting go is a decision that only you can make. The heavier your memories, the more you may need to lighten your load. For some of us, that means physically getting rid of things that continue to remind us of past pain by carting them off to charity or throwing them away. Others of us may find we need to emotionally or mentally disengage from people and possessions by ascribing a different meaning to them.

When you think about it, it is easier to get rid of things than to disengage from your thoughts about them; it is easier to recognize the tangible items in a relationship, like furniture, than the intangibles, like shame, guilt, or anger. In other words, it may be hard to give a sweater to Goodwill, but it's not impossible. Yet it is gut-wrenching and soul-searching to wrestle with inequity or deception, then forgive and walk away.

Tangibles are easier to deal with because they surround us. They are visible reminders of our pain. They also can mirror what we value. The tangibles that I found the hardest to part with were the hand-knit sweaters I had made during the final years of my first marriage. After the divorce, they triggered a memory. I kept seeing myself sitting by the fireplace after work knitting away and wondering why my husband was always working late. One day the memories felt so heavy that I decided to give the sweaters away to somebody who could enjoy them without the pain that I associated with them. In letting them go, I felt freer, and I felt good about the fact that I made somebody else happy.

Right now you may not be in a position to get rid of the tangibles in your life. You may want to keep them for emotional or financial reasons. Maybe you have decided to hold on to a departed child's keepsakes or to stay in the house you lived in with your former spouse. You are letting go of the pain associated with these things and finding new ways to cherish the memories. Whatever way you decide to let go of what reminds you of past pain, you just have to do it. Only you will know what works for you.

Releasing the intangibles takes more time. You have to dig deeper. None of us gladly tackles shame and guilt or whatever's at to the bottom of what provokes us. There were times I thought I couldn't do it—and I didn't want to. It's okay to be reluctant. When we let go of a relationship, we don't always gain closure or get to say the last word. It's hard letting go of our need for validation and approval and to release others to believe what they want. Sometimes, despite our best efforts to let go, we will still experience remembered pain. Like the phantom pains amputees feel in a limb they lost, we will continue to feel emotional pain and relive memories from a lost relationship. That's normal.

But staying stuck is not! If something is holding you back or keeping you stuck, whether it is anger over a failed relationship, fear of the unknown future, or items from the past, loosen your grip. Set yourself free by letting it go. You might find, as I did, that the more you get rid of, the more neutral you feel about the past. The more you are willing to part with, the less you have to lug around, and the more balance you achieve.

PRAYER PAUSE: *Lord, help me let go of whatever is holding me back. I don't want the healing process to take any longer than necessary.*

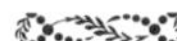

Somehow, when we no longer feel in control,
we become available to deeper aliveness.

RICHARD MOSS

My Mini Journal of Hope and Gratitude

Get rid of all bitterness, rage, anger . . . EPHESIANS 4:31

DATE	I AM ANGRY BUT	WHO I NEED TO FORGIVE

Let It Go

If you are holding on to a past hurt . . .
If someone can't treat you right . . .
If you are angry or vengeful . . .
If you keep judging others . . ..
If you are feeling stressed . . .
Whatever you're trying to handle yourself,
God says, "Take your hands off!"
Let it go..

AUTHOR UNKNOWN

If life was fair, Elvis would be alive and the impersonators would be dead.

JOHNNY CARSON

Elastic Moments

For Reaching Up and Stretching Out

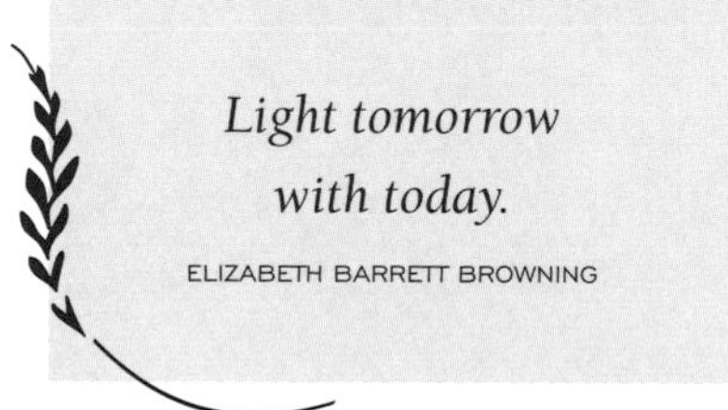

Light tomorrow with today.

ELIZABETH BARRETT BROWNING

57. Finding a three-o'clock-in-the-morning friend

Praise be to the God . . . who comforts us in all our troubles, so we can comfort those in any trouble with the comfort we ourselves have received from God.

2 CORINTHIANS 1:3, 4 NIV

There are times we need a friend we can trust. Someone with whom we can share our private thoughts and secret hurts. Someone who will listen to us, laugh with us, and pray for us. Somebody who knows our flaws yet believes in us anyway. The first year after a major loss is one of those times. But true friends are hard to find.

Pat from Georgia and her husband were only in Atlanta five months when he left her a good-bye note while she was at work. Pat says she didn't have a strong faith, supportive family, or solid friendships to fall back on at the time. "Even learning how to rent an apartment and get a phone hooked up was new to me," she says. "I needed someone to come along with wisdom, support, and encouragement. I needed to be reminded that real life is not cutting off all your hair, impulsively selling your house, or dating men who are jerks just to ease the pain. That only makes you feel better for a few hours." Pat admits that she tended to patch together a life rather than plan it. She didn't buy anything permanent; instead, she waited for something good to happen, thinking things would fall into place after she married again. "I wish somebody would have told me to take some time to find my heart and soul again," she says.

If anyone needed a three-in-the-morning friend, it was Job.

Instead, he had Elihu, Eliphaz, and Bildad, whose advice was as helpful as "ashes" (Job 13:12; 19:13-20) He called them "miserable comforters" with an endless "flow of foolish words" that taunted him instead of helping him (Job 16:2-6). Not only was Job abandoned by his relatives, neighbors, and close friends, but when he insisted on his innocence, his taunting trio refused to reply because they had already determined his guilt (Job 32:1).

Like us, Job didn't need pity or platitudes from his friends but affirmation that his pain was real, and that he was loved and accepted. As his difficulties wore on, Job could have used a wise friend, who had walked in similar shoes and was willing to stick by him while he aired his fears and concerns. No doubt he longed for an encourager to tell him, "*You* are okay, and *you* are going to be okay." During frantic moments when Job said, "The night drags on and I toss till dawn" (Job 7:4), he probably wished someone would say what no one ever had: "Call me anytime–day or night. I am here for you."

During the grieving process, most of us live with a difficult "something or someone" that we do not know how to deal with and do not want to face. A rebellious or hurting child. A harassing ex-husband. A house to sell or a move to make. A car to buy. Employment advice. In these times, we need a human touch to lead the way—holding us accountable to the truth about ourselves and our situation and showing us how to dig out. We also need people in our lives to affirm our shattered worth and to applaud our shaky efforts to make a life.

When I needed help the most, God provided a variety of people. They didn't make decisions for me or pay my bills, but they showed me their scars and encouraged me that I, too, would survive. I am grateful to friends like Al and Mary, who stacked firewood; Charlotte, who helped me shop for a couch; Betty and Yim, who invited me to dinner; MajBritt, who cleaned my kitchen on moving day; Jean and Dick, who crawled under my house to wire my TV; and Eleanor, who volunteered to be my three-in-the-morning friend.

When friends are there for us, letting us babble and sometimes just cry without feeling that they have to fix our difficulties for us, we take charge of our lives again. When others have faith in us, we develop faith in ourselves.

PRAYER PAUSE: *Father in heaven, bring wise, loving friends around me. I appreciate each person You have already sent into my life, even those I only casually know. Help me befriend and encourage others who are hurting. I want to be one of those rare friends who is available anytime—day or night.*

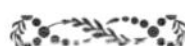

A true friend is someone who is there for you
when he'd rather be anywhere else.

LEN WEIN

58. *Joining up and joining in*

A friend is always loyal, and a brother is born to help in time of need.

PROVERBS 17:17

According to Dr. Dean Ornish, famous for his groundbreaking research and best-selling books on heart disease, the real epidemic we face is emotional and spiritual heart disease—loneliness and isolation. He says we are losing the relationships and intimacy necessary for our survival and healing—the social support that provides us with a sense of connection and community and also the emotional support that gives us a sense of purpose, meaning, and belonging.[48]

But you and I know that at the very time we need social and emotional support the most, we usually avoid it. Simply entertaining the thought of joining a group or making new friends takes time and energy we don't have. We think, *I'll wait until my life settles down to normal.* The danger is that we might not recognize normal if we saw it.

If we wait until all the loose ends are tied up, we will miss opportunities that may not come again, and we put our growth on hold. Even if you aren't where you want to be yet in the grieving process, you are still someone's neighbor and somebody's friend. By closing up your heart, you cut yourself off from the connection and comfort that can help you heal. Sure, a closed heart lessens your risks; but it also narrows your options. Yes, an open heart increases the chance of rejection; but it also broadens the list of those you can involve yourself with, such as people you might meet in a night class or group Bible study or while volunteering. An open heart also gives you opportunity to draw on the friendship and wisdom of your girlfriends.

Columnist Peggy Noonan writes that what we are missing today is girl talk—the private language of women that goes beyond elevated, self-conscious, and self-protected conversation. She says that after the big events in life, like marriage and children, our talk becomes impersonal, a sort of "psychic circling of the wagons." We move from being girls who gab about boys, skirts, and who was popular, to being young women who share "news you could use" about men, relationships, and babies, to being older women who are loyal and discreet—and way too busy to talk.[49]

If women do not talk to each other under normal circumstances, no wonder our isolation increases during times of loss. Perhaps the time has come to rip off our masks of busyness and propriety. Isn't it about time to seek emotional intimacy with each other before our isolation kills us? For me, some of the best conversations I've had in my life happened when I dared to share my spiritual doubts, personal longings, and private fears either in a group setting or a private chat with a girlfriend. Processing information out loud with a friend keeps my gears greased so I don't squeak *too much*. It also broadens my perspective and keeps my motor from burning up.

Research out of Pennsylvania State University shows that when women seek social contact and talk about stressful situations, the hormone oxytocin is released into their system to help them cope. "Engaging in being close to others has anti-anxiety effects," says Laura Cousino, project author. "It calms you down."[50] Dr. Ornish's studies reveal that health and longevity increase, too, when we have social and emotional support.[51]

Another plus of support groups and girlfriends is that when you and I are willing to be transparent about what we have been through, our losses can initiate growth in others. Our openness about life's imperfections can free people to admit their own disappointments and shortcomings. Knowing that we made it *through* our situation helps other believe they will, too. As someone once said, there is no better exercise for strengthening the heart than reaching down and lifting up another.

PRAYER PAUSE: *Lord, help me overcome my reluctance to get involved with others.*

Nothing is so infectious as example.

FRANCOIS DE LA ROCHEFOUCAULD

59. Noticing angels in my midst

He opened the heavens and came down; dark storm clouds were beneath his feet. Mounted on a mighty angel, he flew, soaring on the wings of the wind.

2 SAMUEL 22:10, 11

Have you ever met people who were a sanctuary where you could safely unwrap heartaches, display terror, and unleash tough questions? They generously gave their time and attention but expected nothing in return. They rarely said a word, but somehow their presence was settling and effected a profound change in you. You sensed God's voice in which heart speaks to heart. From then on, you knew exactly what you needed to do, but you were not sure why.

Or what about that accident that didn't happen? You know that your driving skills didn't prevent it. Out of nowhere an invisible hand seemed to hold back your car. You avoided the collision, but you never really knew how. You chalked it up to "a God-thing."

Maybe you have experienced a situation similar to mine. When I learned of my ex-husband's promiscuity, I feared I might be at risk for AIDS and scheduled an exam. A staff nurse escorted me to the open door of an exam room and left. Inside, a tall, broad-shouldered black woman, whom I assumed was another nurse, was straightening supplies. She placed her hand on my shoulder and said, "You are going to be all right," then walked out. After the doctor came and went, I hurried to find her. No one could figure out who I was talking about! And I never saw the woman there again. Today, I can't help but wonder, *Could she have been an angel?* In the midst of that uncertainty, I felt an uncommon peace. And her unconventional prognosis certainly proved right.

The initial trauma of a loss can sometimes quicken the senses. Some people report that the nonessential eroded away and they felt that the eyes of their heart opened to a spiritual dimension they had not noticed before. They sensed a grace and a mystery that in normal circumstances would have eluded them. Later on, they could not prove what both perplexed and sustained them in their time of need.

Whether we call it "a God-thing" or angels in our midst, the sacred is all around us, nudging us toward a deeper-higher-broader relationship with our Creator. God is a much bigger, more mysterious being than we can ever imagine. Romans 11:33 says we cannot begin to comprehend what He is up to. Job says, "He reveals mysteries from the darkness, and brings the deep darkness into light" (Job 12:22).

We know that God created angels. These spiritual beings, imbued with concern for us, have made numerous appearances in human form that are documented throughout the Old and New Testament.[52] They minister to believers by directing their activities and conveying messages; by offering guidance, protection, and deliverance; by comforting and providing for them.[53] The Bible reports angels standing between heaven and earth, wielding swords, baking cakes, pointing out water wells, giving prenatal advice, rolling away tombstones, and sitting in gardens.[54] According to Billy Graham, angels work on our behalf; but because we are not always aware of their presence, they might be our companions or neighbors.[55]

Some people label an unexplained happening or what works out on our behalf a coincidence. Others call it fate. But for me, it is evidence of divine intervention into our ordinary lives.

PRAYER PAUSE: *Creator God, You are so awesome and worthy of praise. Thank you for each time You intervened in my life and I didn't even know it. And thanks for the people in my life who act as Your angels of mercy when I need a human touch.*

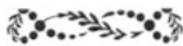

I would rather live in a world
where my life is surrounded by mystery
than live in a world so small that my mind could comprehend it.

HARRY EMERSON FOSDICK

60. Looking around to see how far I've come

Set up road signs; put up guideposts.
Mark well the path by which you came.

JEREMIAH 31:21

Jars filled with pieces of broken beach glass adorn Maggie's kitchen counter. The pieces vary in texture, size, and color, with dark blue glass being the rarest. Some are smooth and sanded. Others are crusted with barnacles. Maggie's favorites are the cracked tops and bottoms of bottles. She says the broken glass awakens memories of the ocean—the sound of waves pounding the shore and the taste of salt in the air. "I'm reminded that beauty comes in different sizes and textures," she says. "You realize that even glass chips, pottery shards, and puzzle pieces have value, especially after you feel like your life has broken into a million pieces."

After her twenty-three-year marriage ended, Maggie, who is a teacher with a master's degree in educational administration, started driving to the coast to think. As she walked alone on the beach, she found a sense of rhythm and continuity. She discovered a primitive peeling away of layers—the expectations and suppositions that don't have any real meaning—and a getting to the core of things. Maggie credits her friend, Linda, who recently died of ovarian cancer, as the one who sparked her interest in collecting beach glass.

Over time, Maggie's beach visits expanded to territory up and down the California and Oregon coastline. The farther she ventured, the greater her confidence. Two days after her daughter married, she flew to New York, treating herself to the theater and dinners, tours of Liberty Island and the Metropolitan Museum of Art, and leisurely strolls through Central Park.

"The wedding was the first time I had spent all day with my ex-husband since our divorce a year earlier," says Maggie. "This trip was my reward for having made it through that day. I also needed something else to look forward to and to know that I could put it together all by myself."

Today Maggie realizes that she has journeyed far from the years she spent in an emotionally and verbally abusive relationship with a man who also physically beat her. She says she is now doing the things her ex-husband would never do or allow her to do. Four more times she has traveled by herself to New York City. She holds season tickets to the San Francisco Symphony. She also took out a mortgage on a townhouse, refinanced her car, and made a major purchase from an art gallery in Carmel, "just for fun without asking anyone's permission"—a two-foot bronze statue of a ballerina that now welcomes friends into her living room. "After I began sharing with people again, my classroom aide taught me to fly a kite, and now I've taught my grandson," she says. "I have finally claimed a life that fits me."

As Maggie looks back on her life, she knows where she got her tenacity from—her own mother. Rose was widowed at age fifty-four, three days before Christmas. Maggie, who was in her late twenties at the time, says her mother told her and her two sisters that their dad was not able to do any shopping that year but that he had put some money aside. She decided he would have been happy if they all went to Disneyland on Christmas Day instead of sitting around mourning. "I've always admired her for doing that," says Maggie. In the years that followed, Rose accepted employment with the county government and eventually retired, then traveled, and today works for the YMCA, where she has been the past fifteen years. "She's an incredible woman. Most of her peers are gone," says Maggie. "She's in her mid-eighties now and she's learning the computer."

Whether you are like Rose, learning new skills at eighty, or like Maggie, finally claiming a life that fits you, it is never too late to be what you might have been. As you look back on your own life and see how far you have come, don't be embarrassed by your brokenness. Let it remind you that beauty comes in different textures, sizes, and colors—and that your life still has value regardless of your age or situation (Isaiah 54:11-14).

PRAYER PAUSE: *Thank you, Lord, for being with me in the past. I know that each experience I have been through has made me a wiser, more tenderhearted woman.*

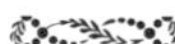

What's past is prologue.

WILLIAM SHAKESPEARE

61. Table for one, please

I trust in God, so why should I be afraid?
What can mere mortals do to me?

PSALM 56:4

Trying to rebuild the confidence we have lost can be unnerving, especially when combined with grieving. On top of losing our confidence, loss often forces us into unfamiliar and challenging situations that we must learn to cope with alone. Yet the paradox is that when we dare to venture out and do things by ourselves, we gain the confidence we need.

There is no better time to start than right now. It is time for breaking with our excuses, mapping uncharted internal terrain, and flexing our willingness to try something new. This is a good time for stretching our attitude and creating the opportunities in which wonderful things can happen. Whatever our circumstances, life is too short to put on hold the experiences God created for our earthly enjoyment and eternal growth.

If we do not make the time and create the occasions where things can happen, no one else will do it for us. As we mull over new situations in our mind, our first attempt may be only a shy look-and-see. Next, we may try a hesitant tippytoe of involvement. As with physical exercise, we only see results through repetitive practice, determination, and discipline. The more we are willing to step over our timidity and beyond our isolation, the greater our physical, mental, and emotional elasticity the next time we try. You will know that the time is right for you to reach up and stretch out to life again when you notice a change of heart, such as:

- The Sunday paper arrives and you mentally window shop through department store ads for a new fall sweater because you can imagine a place where you might wear it.
- A new movie is released and you are dying to see it, but you don't want to wait until it comes out on video.
- The idea of having someone else cook, serve, and do the dishes sounds so irresistible that you don't mind telling a maitre d', "Table for one, please."

Stepping out alone that first year after a loss is not easy for anyone. A lot of us are not only unsure of what others expect of us but of what we expect of ourselves. We may feel guilty just entertaining the thought of laughing again or enjoying ourselves. We wonder what others will think if we suddenly sport a new wardrobe or different makeup. For many of us, the mere idea of sitting alone in a theater or in a symphony hall is a terrifying mental adventure that is difficult to take. A few of us have learned to be wary of church events. Just watching people filing into the sanctuary or fellowship hall reminds us of the loading of the ark. It seems that everyone but us arrives in pairs.

Jennifer, who is recently separated from her husband, says the first time she ventured out to a church event "with all these couples" was awkward. Then, she spotted her friend Sarah, who was alone because her policeman-husband had to work. "I was sad driving home alone, but I didn't fall apart. What made it easier was realizing that I wasn't the only one there who wasn't a couple," says Jennifer.

But what happens when you attend a get-together and discover you *are* the only single person there? Yes, you will feel alone and vulnerable. Take it from someone who risked giving it a try, you will get through this. With time and practice, you will become more self-assured. A loss of confidence can make any of us feel like we stand out in a crowd. To avoid feeling this way, the easiest solution is hole up at home. But this is not the time to stay home, remain isolated, and do nothing. This is the time when you need to reconnect with life. You must dare yourself to do what you need to do and really want to do—even if doing new things feels daunting.

Patricia Avery, a publicist living in Colorado Springs, found herself single again after a divorce. She offers these suggestions whenever you want to dine alone:

- *The first time*: Take along reading material to hide behind, such as a newspaper.
- *The next time*: After you get past the initial angst, sit there acting like you have the same good sense everyone else has and look around the restaurant.
- *Return visits*: Never be afraid to ask the hostess or maitre d' to seat you at a better table, such as one with a window view. Don't settle for a spot along a banquette (booth) unless you prefer it.

PRAYER PAUSE: *God, I know I can do anything if my confidence is secure in You.*

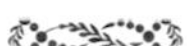

The amount of satisfaction you get from life
depends largely on your own ingenuity, self-sufficiency, and resourcefulness.
People who wait around for life to supply their satisfaction
usually find boredom instead.

DR. WILLIAM MENNINGER

62. Discovering a resilience I never knew

. . . We were under great pressure, far beyond our ability to endure, . . .
But this happened that we might not rely on ourselves but on God. . . .

II CORINTHIANS 1:8, 9 NIV

Many people believe that resilience means bouncing back after life's blows knock you off your feet. But when you think about it, we never bounce back into the same set of circumstances that existed before a loss. We don't necessarily resume being the same person we were either.

Perhaps resiliency is more about grit, grace, and God than it is about rubber. We don't recover from our losses and rebuild new lives because we magically rebound from our losses—but because we transcend them. We transcend them by overcoming our fear of asking for help when we need it. We transcend them by having faith in ourselves, by believing God created us for a reason, and being willing to do what it takes to make our lives work.

But realistically speaking, you and I know that there are times our elastic is shot and we don't have a reserve to draw from. When that happens, we must find the grace to wait it out without giving up or we will block our progress. Instead of letting failure get the best of us, we can learn to roll with the punches until we muscle the inner strength to get up one more time than we are knocked down. That is the benefit of transcendence. It helps us overcome and rise above. But what works for me may not work for you. You see, our resilience is as variable as our God-given uniqueness. It also varies according to our willingness at the moment. Some of us may need time and a multitude of life experiences to develop resilience. Others of us may go a lifetime without ever learning transcendence.

John DeFrain, Ph.D., a professor of family studies at the University of Nebraska who focuses in particular upon resilience, tells the story of a young girl who witnessed her sister being continually slapped by their father for over an hour because she said grace wrong. "I remember sitting there across from her, paralyzed. I just kept praying, 'Get it right,'" the girl says. "The problem was, she was doing it right, just the way we learned it in Sunday school." Dr. DeFrain emphasizes people do not bounce back from horrific mistreatment or abuse, but instead build their own sanctuary and sanity within it and use their adversity as an antidote to make the world better.[56]

Perhaps another component of resiliency is an inner God-given vision and strength that enables us to see through and stretch beyond our circumstances. This eternal perspective functions like a lens through which we can filter what happens to us and find the hope and purpose we need to go on even when our situation looks hopeless and life appears meaningless. Resilient people aren't born tougher, but they are persistent. They envision themselves surviving instead of collapsing. They are willing to seek change and be changed. They aren't afraid to take risks or look at life from a wide-angle telescopic camera, panning out to the worst-case scenario, deciding what they can live with, then pulling back to their present position and taking the next step.

Even if you don't feel resilient right now, the realization that you did not dissolve during the grieving process but survived with soul and sanity intact can give you the inner fortitude you need to ponder that next step. It can reaffirm your faith that God is still working in your life.

When you and I begin to engage more with the present than the past, we start concentrating on what we can do instead of what we have lost. Our priorities become more fine-tuned and we dare to plan for a future, the way Hilary, Marge, and Beth did.

After her sixteen-year marriage ended, Hilary Smith-Wade decided to take a risk and enroll at a local university for a graduate degree in the field of her dreams.

Two years after her divorce, Marge Brown thought she would find a townhouse "just big enough for me." Instead, she broadened her vision by purchasing a larger home than she needed that she makes available to the church ministry team for meetings and uses as a guest house for conference attendees from all over the world.

Beth's husband left and had an affair with an exotic dancer. Although Beth prayed for the marriage to be restored, it never was. But this gutsy nurse imagined herself succeeding. She surveyed the unused space in her house and decided to open its rooms to other women who were hurting and needed a safe place to heal.

In time, with a little grit, a lot of grace, and an infinite God, you, too, can find a way of taking on the losses in your life and coming out the other side. You have more flex in your heart and stretch in your spirit than you think. With your cooperation, you can discover a resilience that you never knew you had.

PRAYER PAUSE: *Heavenly Father, I now know that I have everything I need within me, including the strength and resiliency to recover from my losses and rebuild my life. Help me believe myself when I say, "I can do this!"*

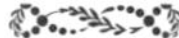

A resilient person works within today's reality while stretching toward tomorrow's possibilities.

KARI WEST

63. *Jesus, how does anybody make it without You?*

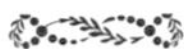

Because I live, you also will live.

JOHN 14:19 NIV

As women we know that the odds are against us. Can't find where I read the numbers, but statistics clearly show most wives outlive their husbands. A third of us have experienced divorce. For many, the inability to conceive is a painful reality. Some of us have birthed babies with congenital disorders, learning disabilities, and emotional-behavioral problems. A few of us have lost children to the drug culture, an eating disorder, a fatal accident, or suicide. Others are facing long-term illness. Few of us will escape burying our parents.

Getting through these times when loss hits home is never easy. Loss defies our understanding, strains our relationships, and riddles our hope for the future. Our understanding of God's providence often falls short, especially when we stumble across verses like Isaiah 43:2-3:

> When you go through deep waters and great trouble, I will be with you. When you go through rivers of difficulty, you will not drown! When you walk through the fire of oppression, you will not be burned up; the flames will not consume you.

Maybe you are thinking, *I don't get it. I* am drowning! *My mind* is *on fire. Pain and suffering consume every waking moment of my day.* You're not alone. A lot of us hang precariously between fire and water, between faith and doubt, looking for a God in scuba gear wielding a fire extinguisher. We want proof—a seeing-is-believing assurance that the Lord of our life is real (John 20:26-29). We long for a God who actively seeks us out instead of remaining quiet and standoffish in a far-off somewhere.

Author Philip Yancey, who wrestled at length with similar thoughts in many of his Gold Medallion Award-winning books, says that is exactly why God sent His one and only Son to earth. Jesus brought God *near* by revealing a loving God "who comes in search of us, a God who makes room for our freedom even when it costs the Son's life, a God who is vulnerable."[57]

Yancey writes that the cross is proof that God uses what makes us feel inadequate and plunders our hope to accomplish His purpose. "On the day we call Good Friday, God defeated sin, routed death, triumphed over Satan, and got his family back," he says.[58] "That dark, Golgothan Friday can only be called Good because of what happened on Easter Sunday, a day which gives a tantalizing clue to the riddle of the universe."[59]

That is why we do not live as those who have no hope (I Thessalonians 4:13). God responds to us from a father's heart. Because He knows how it feels to watch a loved one die, He has *syn pathos* for us; our word *sympathy* means "to feel or suffer with." In the gaping emptiness between yesterday and tomorrow, God is accomplishing His purpose in the universe and in our individual lives—because of what happened on the cross. Jesus Christ bridges the distance from where we are to where our heavenly Father longs for us to be.

Even when the odds are against us and our earthly bodies drown or burn, our eternal soul will live on. However it may appear, God has not abandoned us as we struggle to live between "the time of promise and fulfillment"—between Good Friday and Easter Sunday, what Yancey describes as "Saturday, the day with no name."[60] Only in the struggle can we see tantalizing clues to the riddle of our lives—God's life within us is stronger than death; his light, brighter than the darkness surrounding us.

PRAYER PAUSE: *God, thank you for sending Your Son to die on that cross for me. Help me live with resurrection hope, knowing that you span the empty space between the woman I was before the wound and the woman who is still emerging. Jesus, I don't know how anybody makes it through this life without You.*

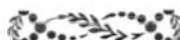

Don't let your wounds interfere with your mission.

STEVE ARTERBURN

My Mini Journal of Hope and Gratitude

. . . the people who know their God
will display strength and take action. DANIEL 11:32 NASB

DATE	ANGELS IN MY MIDST	I AM GAINING CONFIDENCE BY

In forty hours I shall be in battle, with little information, and on the spur of the moment will have to make the most momentous decisions. But I believe that one's spirit enlarges with responsibility and that, with God's help, I shall make them, and make them right. GENERAL GEORGE S. PATTON

The will of God will not take you where the grace of God cannot keep you.
ANONYMOUS

Spirited Moments

For Traveling Lighter and Trusting More

There comes a moment
when you have to stop
revving up the car
and shove it into gear.

DAVID MAHONEY

64. Accepting what is and improving on it

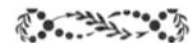

Because of the Lord's great love we are not consumed, for his compassions never fail. They are new every morning; great is your faithfulness. I say to myself, "The Lord is my portion; therefore I will wait for him."

LAMENTATIONS 3:22-24 NIV

Acceptance is one of the best gifts you can give yourself. It is a way of acknowledging that God can and will use for your good and His glory whatever is happening in your life, including loss and suffering. But acceptance is not a let-it-happen sort of thing but a way of being dauntless in the face of life's obstacles. It is also not a wait-and-see proposition but a God-given boldness. Acceptance is a conscious decision and a skill that you must practice.

Many experts claim that acceptance is not necessarily the last step in grief recovery, but, rather, it might be one of the first steps. That is because the brain will continue to fire messages that something is wrong until we acknowledge the messages, reflect on their meaning, and accept the truth that we are in the process of mourning a profound loss. Only after we accept the reality of our situation will the firing cease.

A woman who has experience with acceptance is Joni Eareckson Tada. In writing about accepting her disability, she reminisced about a wintry afternoon when she wished she could jump out of her wheelchair and onto the back of a horse to trek through snowdrifts. Instead, she sadly waved to her sisters as their horses trotted past the window where she was sitting. After dinner that evening, Joni asked her sister, Jay, to wrap her in a blanket and wheel her outside. Alone, Joni listened to wind sighing through pines and watched snowflakes gathering in the creases of her blanket. "My sadness vanished just like the ugly, muddy ruts in the pasture. No, I couldn't ride horseback in the snow, but I could appreciate the pleasure of a snowy evening even while sitting still," she says. "Accepting my wheelchair didn't happen right then and there. That snowy evening was just one in a long series of many days when the Holy Spirit covered my hurt with His gentle grace." [61]

As Joni's story illustrates, acceptance is not denying our situation or idealizing our circumstances. It is positioning ourselves on the opposite side of wallowing in self pity or blaming others. Acceptance frees us to live in the present moment. It is not negating our losses but making a conscious effort to transition beyond them, first, by acknowledging the darkness for what it is—pain, sorrow, suffering, or evil; next, by rising to the light, breathing fresh air, and feeling part of something bigger. Acceptance is not giving up and putting our lives on hold. As Catherine in Pennsylvania tells us, it is daring to regain our freedom to live.

Twenty-five years ago Catherine and her husband received a cuckoo clock as a wedding gift from a cousin in Germany. Years later, her husband quit his job to become the worship leader in a small country church, sending her back to work as an obstetrical nurse. The day he left her for the choir director, the clock quit ticking. Alone with three children, Catherine prayed for seven years for her husband's return, faithfully dusting the clock and thinking that the day he came home the clock magically would start again. But he never returned. He divorced her without her consent and then remarried.

"It's time to move on! I went to Wal-Mart and bought a new, silver clock. Besides, I miss not knowing if the kids are going to be late for school," says Catherine. "If God is not bringing my husband home, I am ready to accept that, although I really wanted my family to be together. But more than that, I want God's will and best. And I'm daring to hope it is possible God will bring a Christian man into my life who will love and cherish me and be committed to a lifelong relationship."

Our Creator is our model for accepting what is. As pastor and family counselor Jeff Klippenes says, "We need to realize that God isn't still sitting in the Garden praying and trusting that the first couple will come back to him. No. He adapted to reality and moved on. Grace says, 'You blew it. Now you get to *do it over*.'"[62]

With each dauntless step forward, we regain our freedom to live in the reality of what is instead of being imprisoned by the past.

PRAYER PAUSE: *Lord, grace me with an extraordinary boldness to accept my situation.*

Acceptance says, "True, this is my situation at the moment. I'll look unblinkingly at the reality of it. But I'll also open my hands to accept whatever a loving Father sends me."

CATHERINE MARSHALL

65. Releasing what isn't anymore

You have done such wonderful things.
Who can compare with you, O God?
You have allowed me to suffer much hardship,
but you will restore me to life again
and lift me up from the depths of the earth. You will restore me
to even greater honor and comfort me once again.

PSALM 71:19-21

It is tough to accept the challenges of change, including ways we are changed. No one wants change or to be changed. We would rather avoid it. But with or without our cooperation, change happens. You and I know that loss accelerates change by making sure that nothing in our lives stays the same. Unfortunately, the greater our resistance to change, the longer it takes to make peace with it.

Maggie (mentioned in chapter 60) had been married for only a couple of years when her father died. Decades later, when the marriage ended and she embarked on a life of her own, she realized how much she missed her father and wished circumstances had been different. "I wondered, had my dad been alive, would my ex-husband have been different? Would I have been stronger to leave such an abusive relationship sooner?" For Maggie, these haunting questions will forever go unanswered. To come to terms with how these lost relationships have changed her life, she made a modification of her own. She gave up her need to know the answers. She decided that claiming the freedom to go on with her life was more important.

Releasing the past and letting it go has nothing to do with

denying our loss or escaping from pain, but everything to do with traveling lighter and trusting ourselves more. It is another way of lightening our load. Instead of carting around a need to know all the answers, we are leaning into life's twists, cooperating with God's gentle nudging as He shows us the turns in the path on the way to where He wants us to go. We are refusing to apologize for the errors in judgment, mistakes, and failures we have made along the way to today. Instead, we recognize them as experiences that, with God's help, can profoundly change us for the better. We now realize that life's journey is never straight and smooth or our choices simple and easy. Yet despite the changing world around us, we are rebuilding our loss-shattered lives on the truth of God's Word that is changeless and on His love that is dependable and eternal.[63]

Some of us are even finding novel ways to make peace with change and with our ever-changing roles. Geraldine Graham in Indiana did just that. Each November for over twenty-one years, this retired nurse, who is now in her mid-eighties, hosted a pre-Thanksgiving dinner for local widows. "These were women who had lost," says Geraldine. "They'd lost husbands, eyesight, hearing, driving privileges, and their health. Some had even lost their ability to walk." She says that each year a few ladies were picked up at the local nursing home by her husband. Over half needed assistance getting in and out of the car. Several needed help being seated at the table or holding the serving bowls. But the majority always requested her tasty turnips and raspberry pie.

"I started this dinner in 1977 in honor of my mother, who lived in Nebraska," Geraldine says. "I always hoped before she died that she could visit us on Thanksgiving, but she wasn't able to." By releasing what was not meant to be, Geraldine made it possible for others living alone to enjoy a holiday meal together. (I'm proud of my mother's legacy! She is my mentor for making peace with change.)

In this world where change is a constant—whether we have unrealized hopes like Geraldine's or unanswered questions like Maggie's—there comes a time when we must leave behind our former life as if it were fabric caught on a barbed wire fence. Without change herding us forward, we might never achieve our God-given potential to bless the world, because our resistance would continue to hold us back.

PRAYER PAUSE: *Heavenly Father, help me leave the past in its place. I don't want to waste today tending to yesterday. I want to make peace with change.*

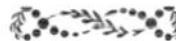

Let nothing disturb you. Let nothing frighten you.
Everything passes away except God.

ST. TERESA OF JESUS

66. *Finding contentment— and liking it here*

Teach me how to live, O Lord. . . . Wait patiently for the Lord. Be brave and courageous.

PSALM 27:11, 14

Oswald Chambers tells us that moods don't go away by praying for them to leave but by kicking them out of our lives.[64] One mood that continually needs a swift boot in my life is discontentment. Instead of being satisfied with what each day brings, I find it all too tempting to complain—even about little things like the weather. But I take comfort knowing that I am not the only one who occasionally gets disgruntled. Lack of contentment seems to come with the territory.

Our dissatisfaction with life goes back to the Garden. Do you really know how Eve was tempted? Satan undermined her contentment! Seduced by a desire for something better—to be as wise as God—Eve fell for Satan's lies. The rest is history (Genesis 3:3-6).

I remember the restlessness I experienced as a result of my divorce, when I moved from a two-story home on a cul de sac to a small house on a busy street. *It's so dark inside and claustrophobic*, I thought. "Ugh, now we have to share a bathroom," my daughter said. There were times I wasn't sure either of us would ever adjust to the cramped quarters, noisy neighbors, or our new lot in life. We missed the dog we had to give away, living next door to people we knew, and a kitchen with room for a regular-sized table and dishwasher. I never got used to storing pots and pans in the garage.

Coming to terms with my situation and learning to like it did not happen overnight. To develop a sense of home in this smaller place meant bidding adieu to excess furniture and taking a flinty-eyed look at everything from small appliances to toys. For me, finding contentment in the midst of a rapidly changing lifestyle was more of a process than a twelve-step plan, more of an act of my stubborn will than an act of worship of God's sufficiency. I struggled with my up-in-arms heart each step of the way—from unpacking boxes to creating closet space. One evening after work I simply decided to plop down on the sofa to let the truth sink in. *I will be content here!* I sighed. Then I flipped open my Bible and read what the apostle Paul said about contentment:

> I am not saying this because I am in need, for I have learned to be content whatever the circumstances. I know what it is to be in need, and I know what it is to have plenty. I have learned the secret of being content in any and every situation, whether well fed or hungry, whether living in plenty or in want. (Philippians 4:11-12 NIV).

My mind surveyed the possessions I had jettisoned. I felt strangely sad and yet oddly liberated. Over time I found myself slowly easing into this smaller new world. I realized through this experience I was gaining the stamina to face anything. I also recognized the reason for my initial resistance. The house wasn't the problem. I was. I am a black-and-white person, hating being thrown into life's grey zones against my will. But loss had forced me here, and it now was teaching me to live within this waiting room—that nebulous timespan between where "loss leaves off" and "new life begins." The loss of my marriage was not the only threat to my well-being. The same snake in the grass that had seduced Eve had also tried to woo me.

Bible commentators say that contentment does not simply mean that our needs are supplied, but that we have an attitude allowing us to be satisfied with whatever is available. This is illustrated in the root word of contentment—*arkeo*, meaning "to be enough," "to be sufficient," "'the acceptance of things as they are' as the wise and loving providence of a God who knows what is good for us, who so loves us as always to seek our good.'"[65]

Wherever loss forces us to live—in poverty or plenty, fullness or hunger, with too much or too little, in a large familiar family home or a small strange house, in good health or in bad—we glorify God when we find our satisfaction in Him.

PRAYER PAUSE: *Lord, give me the grace to adapt to any situation. I want to worship You.*

Since my house burned down, I now own a better view of the rising moon.

MASAHIDE

67. Choosing to see a rainbow in the rain

All around him was a glowing halo, like a rainbow shining through the clouds. This was the way the glory of the LORD *appeared to me.*

EZEKIEL 1:28

I don't know anyone who doesn't like a rainbow. We are fascinated by that overarching band of color that seems to hover in midair between heaven and earth. Sometimes it takes a big storm with a lot of rain before we get to see one. And it isn't much fun if we were stuck outside in the middle of the downpour.

Life's storms also have a way of catching us out in the open and bringing us to our knees. When we are left with a bundle of drenched hopes, it's hard to hold up our heads and believe that there really *is* a rainbow in life's blustery wind, gloomy clouds, and frightening thunder squalls. There are times we can't imagine hope existing, let alone penetrating our darkness.

But it is there. Alice Somers remembers driving down the Pacific Coast Highway near her home in Huntington Beach, California, several years ago after work at a time when she didn't believe her husband would ever stop abusing alcohol. "All of a sudden, you could see forever, all the way to Catalina Island. The air was clear and in the background was the most gorgeous sunset," she said. "And there was a Mozart symphony on the radio as well, and I thought, 'My husband is going to be all right; and even if he isn't, I have this beautiful moment.'" Alice describes the experience as a mini cloud lifting. That feeling stayed with her for a long time. "It was definitely heaven sent," Alice said.

Many of us experience similar epiphanies of hope when we see rainbows, perhaps because their appearance is reflected from the storm itself. They trigger an innate longing within us to push past the darkness in our lives, to live above its shadows, and to look for a flicker of hope.

No wonder the rainbow has become a sign of God's love and a witness of His faithfulness and mercy. A rainbow appears in the part of the sky opposite the sun at the very moment that light passes through the raindrops and is refracted and reflected by the sun's rays. For me, this makes it a perfect metaphor for light shining through darkness.

A rainbow is also a symbol of God's glory, His bright and flaming splendor, the unveiling of His beauty and presence. It is first mentioned in Genesis 9:12-17 as a sign of God's covenant promise that He will never again destroy the world by flood. *Qeshet* is the Hebrew word meaning "bow in the clouds, rainbow, or bow"—an instrument of divine wrath with its arrows, e.g., lightning, thunderbolts, rain. The prophet Ezekiel (1:28) and the disciple John (Revelation 4:3; 10:1) see the rainbow around the throne of God's judgment as manifesting His glory and signifying His mercy and grace. [66]

A rainbow reminds us that God really does mean what He says. He never breaks His promises. The book of Revelation says that Christ *will return* in clouds—not the billowy fluffy kind, but in clouds of fire called the Shekinah glory, representing the presence of God, like the cloud that led the children of Israel out of Egypt and surrounded the Holy of Holies. God is also present in the clouds that overshadow our lives. But we must choose to see Him with childlike faith, the faith of the little girl in this story:

Amber walked daily to and from school. Though the weather this particular morning was questionable and clouds were forming, she made her trek to the elementary school. As the afternoon progressed, the winds whipped up, along with thunder and lightning. The child's mother, concerned that Amber would be frightened and possibly harmed by the storm, got into her car and drove along the route to school to pick her up. As she did so, she saw her little daughter walking along happily; but at each flash of lightning, Amber would stop, look up, and smile. Stopping the car, the mother called to the child to get in the car. As they drove home, Amber continued to turn toward each lightning flash and smile. The mother asked, "What are you doing?" Amber answered, "Well, I must do this because God keeps taking pictures of me."[67]

PRAYER PAUSE: *Lord, although You are veiled in mystery, You renew my faith with the sign You send after each rain. I know You are holding my picture close to your heart.*

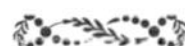

The way I see it, if you want the rainbow,
you gotta put up with the rain.

DOLLY PARTON

68. Seizing the life beyond the loss

Now choose life, so that you and your children may live. . . .
For the Lord is your life, and He will give you many years in the land. . . .

DEUTERONOMY 30:19, 20 NIV

In the natural order of things, we expect to bury our parents, but never our children. Perhaps that is one of the reasons why the death of an innocent baby, in a miscarriage or abortion, creates an agonizing grief. For the rest of your life, you will think about that child every single day. This is a loss people seldom talk about and few understand.

Women who have miscarried say their grief is often discounted. Others make their pain worse with insensitive comments like—"You're young. There's plenty of time to try again," or "It's not as bad as losing a real baby. You weren't that far along."

An abortion also brings its own private grief. Many women who have aborted admit they carry a secret shame. Wherever you stand on the issue, realize not all of the women who consent to aborting their baby do so as a result of selective reduction or because having a child interferes with their lifestyle. That is why Joy shares her story.

When she became pregnant, Joy was a junior in high school. She had a serious boyfriend, with whom she had been intimate for about a year. They had plans to marry and together broke the news of the baby to her parents. "When my mom told us, 'This is not going to happen,' I thought she meant we couldn't get married," says Joy. "The next day she took me to a clinic to be examined. When the doctors told me I wasn't pregnant, but simply needed a routine procedure for my period to start again, I trusted them." She was told the procedure would unblock her fallopian tubes.

Two years later, while walking with a girlfriend, Joy was handed a Right-to-Life pamphlet showing a photograph of an aborted fetus and realized that the "clinic" had been an abortion mill. "I cried for months whenever I would see, hear, or think about a baby," she says. "I was angry with my mom, angry with the clinic, and angry with my ex-boyfriend because he left me. I felt as if my baby had been murdered."

For twenty-two years, Joy stuffed her feelings. When she accidentally ran into the ex-boyfriend in a coffee shop and they had a chance to talk about the past, she learned he had tried to contact her, but that her parents had told him that Joy did not want to see him. "Here we sat, both of us having been through terrible marriages that may not have had to exist, all because of the deceit of the abortion clinic and my parents, who believed they were doing what was best for me," she says.

Perhaps you are also grieving lost years, the way Joy is. Someone you trusted altered the course of your life. You see more years behind you than ahead of you and very little life left to seize. You have forgiven the one who hurt you, yet you feel wounded and wronged anew as memories wash over you. As Lewis Smedes says, "Forgiving does not remove our scars any more than a funeral takes away all of our grief."[68]

Joy can tell you that faith in God does not remove the consequences of others' deceit or manipulation either, but that we do become wiser and we can use that wisdom to help others. As a result of her experience, Joy, who is now a teacher in a Christian high school, often walks hand-in-hand with pregnant girls to break the news to their mothers. She has reconciled with her parents and recently ordered a plaque to be placed in her child's honor at the National Memorial for the Unborn in Chattanooga,

Tennessee. In remembering the wounds and wrongs of her past, Joy is also being honest with herself. "Premarital sex, not the baby, was the sin," she says. "God forgave me for the abortion. But this murder and the suffering behind it has been a horrible price to pay. My baby was not a mistake but a life, who was a surprise and a blessing from the Lord. I think about [my baby] every day and live with hope that someday I will see my baby in heaven."

As we bring our secrets out into the light and trust God to use our scars, we begin to view them not so much as proof of our human failing but as evidence of His gracious healing. They are our credibility badges to enter a hurting world longing to be graced with the compassion and wisdom of our experience.

PRAYER PAUSE: *Lord, I want to seize the life beyond my loss. I am willing to use what I've been through to help others heal.*

To gain that which is worth having
it may be necessary to lose everything.

BERNADETTE DEVLIN

69. Discovering my own reason to keep going

I am counting on the Lord; yes, I am counting on him.
I have put my hope in his word.

PSALM 130:5

Ever think about what moves you to get up in the morning or what passion gets you through the drudgery of the day? Not what motivates your friends or your pastor. But *your* reason. Discovering your own reason to keep going is not as difficult as you think. You must look deep within your heart for clues.

Yet when we are grieving, we often feel there's nothing to look forward to, so we drift away from social activities and educational pursuits that we once enjoyed. The creative side of us shuts down as we put hobbies and home projects on hold. The more our confidence erodes, the less competent we feel. Before we know it, we see an empty shell in place of the vibrant person we used to be. No wonder God teaches us to base our identity on who He is, not on how we see ourselves; on the stability of His love, not on our transient relationships; on His faithfulness, instead of on how we think we are doing.

Experts define self-esteem as the extent to which we accept, love, trust, and respect ourselves. Yet for many of us, the word *self* conjures up visions of someone who is self-absorbed or self-centered. Because we are taught to not talk about ourselves too much or think of ourselves too highly, we bury our uniqueness beneath a layer of self-effacement.

I appreciate the way the poet Robert Browning brings self-esteem into proper perspective. He says, "My business is not to remake myself, but make the absolute best of what God made." Having self-esteem is not synonymous with being selfish, but one way to honor our God-given uniqueness. Only when we find the source of our identity in God can we truly accept, trust, respect, and love ourselves. Then, when the going gets tough, a healthy esteem of self will give us the boost we need to forge ahead.

"When people go at their lives or their jobs with positive feelings about their competence, they're much more willing to try new things and to proceed in the face of failure," says Dr. Barbara Ilardi, a psychology professor at the University of Rochester.[69]

Martha Kostyra is an example of proceeding in the face of failure. She has had more than her share of lost relationships, burnt toast, and mildewed roses. The eldest daughter in a large Polish-Catholic family, she put herself through college with a partial scholarship and a modeling job. In 1976, she started a catering business with a friend; but when the partnership dissolved, she forged ahead. A decade later, she had created a million-dollar empire. Then in 1987, her husband of twenty-six years left her while she was on a book tour for *Weddings*, but she still kept going. Today, Martha Stewart is a household name, with a national television audience of more than two million viewers. What moves Martha is a love for cooking that she discovered as a child.[70]

Granted, the majority of us don't have it in us to create an empire. It's not our thing. But each one of us can discover our own reason to go on. What we love to do can rekindle our passion for life.

To find what moves you, ask yourself: What provides meaning and tranquility to my day? Is there one thing that I always wanted to learn that would provide a sense of accomplishment, build my confidence, and enable me to absorb the shocks of life? Then, look around you. Explore your home and hobbies. Think about the music and literature you like. And don't overlook the garden, which is my all-time favorite hobby. I am glad Martin Luther said, "Even if I knew that tomorrow the world would go to pieces, I would still plant my apple tree." And I can relate to St. Augustine, who was working in his garden one morning when asked about his plans should Christ return that night. He replied, "I would finish hoeing my garden."

Not only can *the thing that moves you* become the reason you get up in the morning, but it can be the driving force that gets you through difficult days ahead and the spark that spurs you on for the rest of your life. It can help you see obstacles as opportunities and enable you to create a challenge out of a catastrophe. As you ride out life's shock waves, it can buoy your spirit, bringing simple enjoyment to the most ordinary moments and making even your worst days worthwhile.

PRAYER PAUSE: *Lord, teach me to accept, love, trust, and respect the unique person You created me to be. Grace me with Your presence as life's challenges and opportunities take me where You want me to be.*

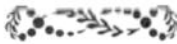

Life is not the way it's supposed to be.
It's the way it is.
The way you cope with it is what makes the difference.

VIRGINIA SATIR

70. *Father, how can I not trust You for what's ahead?*

We depend on the Lord alone to save us. Only he can help us, protecting us like a shield. In him our hearts rejoice, for we are trusting in his holy name. Let your unfailing love surround us, Lord, for our hope is in you alone.

PSALM 33:20-22

It seems that God often asks us to trust Him when the destination is uncertain, when the task outweighs us, and when we feel the most insignificant. I mean, why can't the Lord of the universe toss a couple of extra *Trusty Biscuits* our way so we can hoard a few and make this faith thing less of a struggle? Then, when our spirit needs fortification, we could simply grab a morsel off the shelf, sink our teeth into it, and go on our way. After all, God showered the children of Israel with manna in the wilderness.

Of course, some of those folks acted the way many of us do. They didn't get the main point of the bread-from-heaven demonstration at first, either. Instead of limiting their daily gathering of manna to two omers[71] as God had instructed, some gathered more and others picked up less. The frugal group discovered they had enough to eat. But by morning, the greedy group found that they had nothing left over except a rancid mass of maggots. No wonder God's provision always comes with the clear instruction to trust Him!

For those of us wandering in the wilderness of loss, trust is also a major issue and a huge hurdle. On a day-to-day basis, it is tough to trust God's timing, let alone His sovereignty. We settle for maggots because it is hard to wait patiently *for hope* of what we cannot see (Galatians 5:5).[72] Perhaps most difficult is relying on God for our moment-to-moment needs. It is much easier to point fingers at God for creating maggots in the first place.

Last evening, when I took my dogs for a walk, I stopped off at Starbucks for a cup of coffee on the way. During our stroll I kept mulling over the words of a poster I had noticed on their wall—*New discoveries demand a leap of faith.* I thought back to the early months of my divorce, when Elizabeth Larsen, the pastor's wife, asked me how I was coping. I remember telling her, "I am falling off a cliff, yet I feel like I'm suspended in mid air. There's netting all around me, but the open spaces are large enough for me to slip through them. It's like I am trusting God to catch me before that happens."

Trust is a lot like leaping before you look. I Peter 1:8 says, "Though you do not see him, you trust him." Unless you and I have confidence that God will catch us if we fall, we will never perch on the edge of new discoveries, and we certainly won't jump. That is why we need to look back on past situations in our lives and make mental notes of the occasions when God was with us. If we can hold on to evidence of His presence in the past, we will have something to fall back on in the here-and-now, when darkness obscures the way forward and we can't see where to step.

Philip Yancey puts it this way: "The kind of faith God values seems to develop best when everything fuzzes over, when God stays silent, when the fog rolls in. . . . Fidelity involves learning to trust that, out beyond the perimeter of fog, God still reigns and has not abandoned us, no matter how it may appear."[73]

PRAYER PAUSE: *Lord, I know You were there with me in the past. How can I not trust You for the unknown future?*

Hope for the best. Expect the worst.
Then take what God gives you.

DR. JAY HALAP, EMERGENCY ROOM PHYSICIAN

My Mini Journal of Hope and Gratitude

. . . God can be trusted to keep his promise. HEBREWS 10:23

DATE	I AM TRYING TO ACCEPT	I FELT GOD'S PRESENCE WHEN

The word crisis originates in the Greek word krines, *meaning "the parting of the ways." In the wake of a major crisis, we nearly always part ways with our past view of reality—whether we do it willingly or kicking and screaming.*

GLORIA KARPINSKI

A ninety-seven-year-old woman died. In her will she left these explicit instructions: "No male pallbearers. If they didn't take me out when I was alive, they aren't going to carry me out when I'm dead!"

AUTHOR UNKNOWN

Glorious Moments

for Simply Celebrating Life

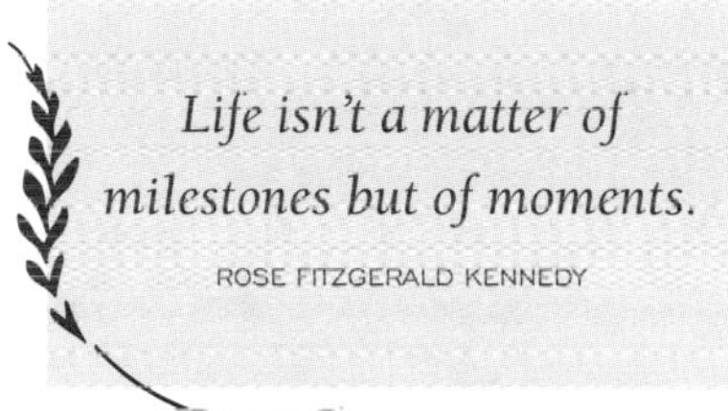

Life isn't a matter of
milestones but of moments.
ROSE FITZGERALD KENNEDY

71. Graced by simple things

The steps of the godly are directed by the Lord.
He delights in every detail of their lives.
Though they stumble, they will not fall,
for the Lord holds them by the hand.

PSALM 37:23-24

So often, we get so involved with living that we forget to live. Yet only a step or two away from our complex lives—that stack of unpaid bills, the sheets to be changed, and the unanswered mail—are simple things that can flood our minds with wonder and fill our hearts with joy. Simple things lie all around us in the routine of our everyday—the soft bed we sleep in and running water. They can also be found in the unpretentious world of nature that awaits our discovery. What is plain and commonplace liberates us to rejoice in and to enjoy God's gracious provision. Simple things give us the clarity to put our complicated lives into proper perspective.

This morning I needed clarity, so I wandered outside to my garden with a mug of coffee and my Bible. I have ventured out here quite often during the writing of this book. Sitting among the garden's greeneries has a way of settling my thoughts and taking me to the heart of what I want to say.

It was the same today. Visible all around me was the simple abundance of God's gracious provision. I saw it in a bowed and bent sunflower head heavy with seed, in lettuce lying languid in the warm sun, and in the dainty goldfinch sipping water from a leaky faucet. Even the worm-holed rose leaves dusted with mildew proclaimed God's goodness as loudly as the fragrance of honeysuckle riding the breeze and the ripened pears dotting the ground.

In those sacred moments, the sights, smells, and sounds of earth graced my senses. These are simple things that I don't deserve, didn't earn, can't buy, and often walk right past. Simple things that inundate my whole being with wonder, beauty, and joy. Simple things that evidence a Divine Creator who faithfully provides for His creation through one season after another (Romans 1:20). Perhaps the hymn writer Isaac Watts described it best with these timeless words he wrote in 1784: "There's not a plant or flower below, But makes Thy glories known."[74]

Wherever you live and whatever your surroundings, simple things are all around you. You don't need a garden to see them, but it is the most marvelous place to look. Moments of joyful simplicity can be found in the cool, springy lawn of a nearby city park, in the welcoming adoration of a pet, and in a juicy bowl of fresh fruit. They wait in the crisp, clear darkness of a wintry night when you realize that the Creator of the whole universe is peeking at you through trillions of twinkling stars.

You can rejoice in and enjoy God's simple abundance whether or not the sheets get changed. So put off opening the mail. Tell those bills to wait—well, maybe not the bills. But you get the picture. A demanding world will always be clamoring for our total attention. Unless we see our complicated lives from a higher perspective, we will remain its prisoners.

"[Simplicity] is an inward spirit of trust," explains Richard Foster. "We are dependent upon God for the simplest elements of life: air, water, sun. What we have is not the result of our labor, but of the gracious care of God. . . . Simplicity means the freedom to trust God for these (and all) things."[75]

PRAYER PAUSE: *Creator God, thank you for gracing my life with a wealth of simple things. Open my eyes to Your glory and help me celebrate being alive. I want to live each day with gratitude for what I take for granted—fundamentals of my every day that many people around the world can only dream about. Food in the refrigerator. Running water and an indoor toilet. A hot shower and a soft bed.*

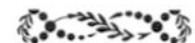

The best things are nearest:
breath in your nostrils, light in your eyes,
flowers at your feet, duties at your hand,
the path of God just before you.

ROBERT LOUIS STEVENSON

72. That man whistled at me!

Let the smile of your face shine on us, Lord. You have given me greater joy than those who have abundant harvests of grain and wine. I will lie down in peace and sleep, for you alone, O Lord, will keep me safe.

PSALM 4:6-8

I'm glad God likes surprises, because so do I. Not only does God know exactly what we need, but He knows when we need it the most. Sometimes he surprises us with a friend's words of encouragement or, when we least expect it, along comes a wave, a whistle, or a phone call that can make our day. If it is from the right kind of man, we might even start thinking about swooning again.

That's what happened to Eunice. After being widowed for eighteen years, she found love again only a block from her house. She couldn't have been more surprised. You see, Bob, his wife, Mildred, and their children had been her neighbors for years. They had shopped at the same market and attended the same church. After Mildred discovered she had terminal cancer, she asked Eunice for prayer. "You're the only one I know who will pray for me," she told Eunice. She also asked her to take care of the food for friends and relatives who would be stopping by after her funeral.

To Eunice's surprise, five months after Mildred passed away the telephone rang. It was Bob, asking her for a lunch date. Afterwards, he said, "Well, the lunch went all right. Now we should go out for dinner." Dates to musicals and trips to the art museum followed. Then, one glorious October morning, while Eunice was watering her front lawn, Bob dropped by and proposed.

"Kind of quick, isn't it?" Eunice replied.

"Well, at our age, we can't wait too long." He wondered if a Halloween wedding date was too soon.

On the fourth day of the new year, they married and then enjoyed fourteen years together. Bob passed away after a long battle with Parkinson's disease, and now Eunice cares for her forty-six-year-old daughter, who was diagnosed with melanoma. "God gives you strength to go through what you have to," Eunice says. "You can't have everything perfect. You have to risk it. Even if you only have a year together, it's worth it. Why, just last week my eighty-one-year-old cousin told me she was getting married and I screamed for joy."

Whatever your age, love might be only a wave, whistle, or phone call away. Don't overlook life's short, sweet surprises (and the tall, handsome ones) that may come your way. There are some kindhearted gentlemen out there, who brake for squirrels and make the world a better place.

If it's the desire of your heart to marry, don't talk yourself out of it. Take a risk. Open yourself to love, whether it be a first or second time around. Even if you don't see it in the picture for yourself right now, who says it is impossible? Only God knows for sure. Let the possibility of new friendships and great relationships put zip in your step.

You see, enthusiasm is contagious, so start your own epidemic. Infect the world around you with your exuberance for living. It may take you some place you've never been. When you feel like a million, you start looking like a million; then, acting like you deserve a million; and soon you begin to attract the friendships and relationships that are one in a million.

Meanwhile, never forget that you already possess the most enduring love of all. Your God delights in you, and He is the one and only Lover who will never leave you (Isaiah 62:2-5).

PRAYER PAUSE: *Lord, I am so glad You take notice of me. Today, I celebrate Your love for me. I am rejoicing in the thought that in Your eyes I'm not half of a lost relationship—but I am whole!*

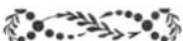

Inspirations never go in for long engagements;
they demand immediate marriage to action.

BRENDAN FRANCIS

73. Taking pleasure in what's whimsical

You have turned my mourning into joyful dancing,
You have taken away my clothes of mourning and clothed me with joy,
that I might sing praises to you and not be silent.
O Lord my God, I will give you thanks forever!

PSALM 30:11-12

Our Creator set a limit to the season of grieving. While we will always *live with* the memory of those we have lost, we do not have to *live in* the pit of bereavement for the remainder of our earthly lives. Not only is our grief healed by the future hope that we will be reunited with our loved ones in heaven, but by the immediate hope that when mourning ends, new music begins.

But how do we begin to hear this music? Is it like listening to a Mozart CD while a low-rider next to us vibrates our car with a rap beat? When we have a hole in our heart, being clothed with joy seems as unlikely as spinning straw into a slinky gold lamé dress.

During times when loss circles back to get the best of me, my outlook brightens again if I can find something to make me smile. A little whimsy can lift my spirit and take away the lump in my throat. Whimsy evokes a sigh of relief, releases a clenched jaw, soothes a furrowed brow—it take an anxious mind off problems.

Whimsy is whatever you want it to be. It is anything and everything ludicrous, eccentric, and quaint that gives you pause. Whatever is good for a laugh is whimsical, whether it's witty, comical, or downright hysterical. It also can be something capricious and flitting that takes you on a wild goose chase until you take yourself less seriously. Whimsy is like the ruffles of frosting around a cake, the sparkling bubbles in apple cider, and the flair of sizzling fajitas. It can be one simple flourish you add to your surroundings that enables you to forget a topsy-turvy day.

When I first brought whimsy home, it was during my most desolate days of bereavement. I felt deprived of the marriage I had thought would last a lifetime. I needed a change but I wasn't sure what or how to do it, so I started slowly with the color peach. While I'm not a peach person or someone who usually indulges in trends that only last a season, I went for this faddish color anyway. Deep in my heart I knew that at this time in my life I needed the elation that comes with feeling frivolous and in vogue.

My first purchase was an inexpensive flowerpot shaped like a shell. Soon I had a peachy throw pillow lounging on the couch. But what really lightened my heart (and my wallet) was splurging on a peach-colored set of towels edged with ribbons and ruffles. During that year of feeling down in the dumps, an ordinary shower became a real treat. By indulging in a little whimsy, I learned that my sense of humor was still intact. You see, I am not a ribbon and ruffle person either, but whimsy won me over by distracting me. My need to take myself less seriously took me down a lighter road. If I had to do it over, I would go there again.

You, too, can put whimsy to work for you. Redecorate your surroundings and allow yourself to play. Take it from one who knows—with a little time and a touch of whimsy, your mourning can turn into dancing just as the psalmist said it would.

PRAYER PAUSE: *Lord, it's time to celebrate life. Show me how to bring closure to my grief so I can get into the swing of things again.*

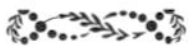

When the situation is desperate,
it's too late to be serious. Be playful.

EDWARD ABBEY

74. *Sure feels good coming home to who I am*

Lord, remind me how brief my time on earth will be. Remind me that my days are numbered, and that my life is fleeing away.

PSALM 39:4

There is no place on earth quite like your own home. Home offers sanctuary after a long journey or a weary day. Here, you can let your hair down and be real. Home provides a safe place for facing fears and discovering dreams—a place of solace, renewal, and respite from grief. It is where you belong.

But home is more than a house. It is also a sacred place deep within you. Here, in the core of your being, God's spirit witnesses to yours. In this abode, love abides and you are satisfied, because God is enough. Though you still have anxious days and restless nights, you are not alone in this place. You keep coming home to who you are in God, knowing you belong wherever He is.

But are you at home in your own skin? In our media-driven culture that downplays maturity and glamorizes youth, not many of us are. Maybe you fret about crows' feet and sagging skin. As women, we feel pressured to look younger than we are because now we have products and procedures to make it happen. We open a magazine and out pop anti-aging messages coaxing us to believe that youth comes from a surgeon's knife or in a bottle. We pass a cosmetic counter and what jumps out at us? Skin renewal cream. Age-defying lotion. Anti-wrinkle serum. A rainbow of hair color products. No wonder we feel uncomfortable with wrinkled skin and gray hair. Somewhere along the way we have lost the distinction between looking our best and obsessing over our looks.

Let's face it—we can't stop time from altering these physical containers in which we live. We blink and suddenly, we've lost our contours. We look in the mirror and see our parents looking back. Unexpected illness or injury can steal our looks and rob us of vigor. This is especially disturbing in a society with plenty of room for the young and the beautiful but where aging is unacceptable, the elderly are invisible, and talk about death is taboo.

When Caroline Stevens' mother was diagnosed with Alzheimer's disease and her father developed Parkinson's disease, she found herself not only grieving their mortality but coming to terms with her own. "One of the things I miss with my Mom is the conversations. She talks, but I can't expect any more mother-daughter counsel," Caroline says. "While I can still deny my own aging with a little hair dye and makeup, I am waiting for my Mom to say, 'Carol, who?' This is something I can't fix cosmetically."

In the same way that we come home to who we are in our earthly house, we can come home to our own skin. We do not have to lose our way. We can live authentically and fully in each place. In mourning the physical deterioration and loss of those we love, we can begin the process of accepting our mortality by putting aging in its proper perspective, as Caroline is doing.

Our aging skin is not the totality of who we are. It does not reflect our inner beauty, because true beauty goes beyond the shape of our nose and the slope of our breasts. It is not synonymous with the promised hype on cosmetic labels.

According to Kerry Walters, professor of philosophy at Gettysburg College, early Western thinkers understood beauty differently. He explains, "If God is the source of beauty in the natural order, and if natural beauty possesses wholeness, harmony, and radiance, then these three qualities must be supremely present in God. God isn't just the First Artist, Creator of the *kosmic* masterpiece. God is also *the* masterpiece, Beauty itself."[76]

Since we reflect God's image, we are more than a smooth or wrinkled face, firm or flabby thighs. We are beautiful because the Creator of our soul is eternal beauty. As Caroline mentions, "We forget we're living here temporarily. Because we doubt the eternal, we strive to hold on to our youth, thinking it is the sure thing."

Both Caroline and I admit that we struggle with our mirror image. She resents having to masquerade as younger to maintain a competitive edge in the job market. I question my decision to go gray. Neither one of us relishes the idea of being invisible. We welcome the wisdom of age, but we also grieve the loss of youth. And we long to be like the grandmothers we remember who were happy growing older. They modeled not only acceptance of their mortality but how to be at home with their natural selves.

Home is where you and I belong. Just as you struggled to find your way home to your earthly house and your eternal spirit, you can find your way home to your own skin. Don't let the journey terrify you. Rather, discover that place of looking your best without obsessing over your looks. Remember that God already put out the welcome mat. It says: *She Who Is Forever Beautiful Lives Here.*

PRAYER PAUSE: *Lord, help me acknowledge life's brevity and accept the loss of my youth. I know that each loss is leading me into a more authentic relationship with You. Teach me to age gracefully. With each breath I take, may I reflect Your truth, goodness, and beauty. Keep reminding me that I belong to You—the restorer, who already conquered eternal death—and that a new body waits for me in heaven. (P.S. Let me know if You need suggestions about the size.)*

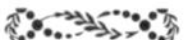

A person travels the world over in search of what he needs,
and returns home to find it.

GEORGE MOORE

75. Is this really me giggling?

There is a time for everything. . . . a time to heal. . . . a time to laugh.

ECCLESIASTES 3:1, 3, 4

Jeanne Satre knows how to laugh. Perhaps it's her enjoyment of humor that enabled her cope with the birth of twin boys and the adoption of two girls from Korea, another girl from her hometown, and several more from Mother Teresa's orphanage in India. Four are orthopedically challenged and one has muscular dystrophy. Her personal story of how God enlarged her heart for these children, helped her confront her own adoption issues, and deal with breast cancer makes you cry, but it also makes you laugh.[77]

Jeannie is just that way. She weaves humor into the Bible studies she teaches, into women's conference workshops, and, most of all, into her life. She e-mails jokes to her friends. I enjoy her light side because it helps me to lighten up. Do you know that humor has these profound effects on our bodies?

- Distracts you from pain by releasing endorphins that make you feel better and more alert.
- Increases blood circulation, lowers blood pressure, relieves muscle tension, eases stress, and makes you more relaxed.
- Revs up the body's ability to fight infection and clears mucus from your lungs.[78]

No wonder it is so important to look on the lighter side of situations, to laugh at our fumbles and failures, and to use humor in deflecting anger and dealing with conflict. Norman Cousins wrote, "The tragedy of life is not death but what dies inside a man while he lives." He understood the healing power of humor. During bouts of crippling arthritis, he nursed himself back to health by watching Marx Brothers movies and reruns of "Candid Camera." He claimed that a good belly laugh raised his pain threshold and gave him two hours of pain-free sleep.[79]

New research reveals that humor can do wonders for us when we grieve. Dr. Dacher Keltner, associate professor of psychology at the University of California–Berkeley, studied people whose spouses had died six months earlier. They were people who had little reason to laugh. Although most psychologists consider the display of positive emotions during grief to be pathological, Dr. Keltner discovered that with the mourners he interviewed, those who had a tendency to laugh or smile showed less depression and anxiety two to four years later. "Laughter is a healthy mechanism," he says. "It allows you to disassociate yourself from the event so you can engage in more healthful and social emotions."[80]

Don't be embarrassed by what tickles your funny bone. Chuckle over babies spitting bubbles. Grin at your ability to repeat a joke—and remember the punch line. You will feel better if you can laugh at your mistakes and smile through what ails you.

PRAYER PAUSE: *Lord, as the words of Psalm 126:1-3 express, You have done great things for me and I am glad. I can't believe that I have looked adversity straight in the face and I'm catching myself giggling again. Proverbs 17:22 says, "A cheerful heart is good medicine." How I need more of this divine prescription that You have provided to heal my grieving heart!*

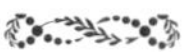

The mere absence of any major problems at the present should be a cause, in and of itself, for euphoria.

ANONYMOUS

76. I believe I'm really going to be okay

We are pressed on every side by troubles, but we are not crushed and broken.
We are perplexed, but we don't give up and quit.
We are hunted down, but God never abandons us.
We get knocked down, but we get up again and keep going.

II CORINTHIANS 4:8, 9

How many times these past months have you encountered a boulder in your way when you thought the road was finally clear? Today, one looms in front of me. I have writer's block. I have been sitting in front of my computer forever, longing to look through a window instead of staring at a screen. Not only are the words not flowing but I'm stuck inside a house with shades drawn, listening to the whirl of fans. It's 100 degrees out side, way too warm to go looking for inspiration in my garden.

For now, the only way I can scale this boulder is by believing this setback is temporary, that I will manage to get through the day, and that I'm really going to be okay. From past experience, I know the heat will end, the writer's block won't last, and someday I will hold my new book in hand.

The block that I encountered in my writing is similar to the blocks of frustration we run into with grief. We think we have figured things out and we're on our way; then we hit a boulder. We begin to wonder if we have made any progress at all. It feels like we haven't budged an inch. We wander in circles, turning the same corners, climbing up and falling back, forever encountering obstacles. We are exhausted from facing our doubts and fears, creating solutions, and anticipating the future. And we are fed up with setbacks.

Sound familiar? Then, you already know the way up and over. This time around, you are drawing on your past experiences, encouraged that you won't stay stuck. Your heart is in the journey, so you push on, reframing your present situation with future hope. Frustration and despair may loom large for a season, but you know that it won't last. God has not abandoned you. In time, you will be able to see the obstacle for what it is; and, Lord willing, after its season has passed, life will get back to normal.

From time to time everyone encounters these blocks of frustration and despair. The apostle Paul did. After his conversion on the road to Damascus, he encountered incredible obstacles. He lost his possessions and comforts and he faced unpopularity and incarceration, but he didn't give up, give in, or give way to hopelessness. There were probably moments when Paul doubted his progress just as we do. Yet, in his second letter to Timothy, Paul wrote that he had fought the good fight, finished the course, and kept the faith (II Timothy 4:7). We can, too.

When we realize that the daily battle is the Lord's, we can confront the boulders that are in our way. Ask yourself: *What am I going to do about this? Do I cry or slam my fist on the table? Go crazy? Quit my job? Pack up the computer? Adopt out the kids? Or do I finish the course, believing I am really going to be okay?*

PRAYER PAUSE: *Lord, when I'm stopped dead in my tracks by another boulder, help me to remember You're at the top, ready to give me a hand up. Help me to redirect my thoughts toward You. I don't want to squander the moment in front of me.*

Times of stress and difficulty are seasons of opportunity when the seeds of progress are sown.

THOMAS F. WOODLOCK

77. *Lord, I don't want to miss Your plan!*

"My thoughts are completely different from yours," says the Lord. "And my ways are far beyond anything you could imagine."

ISAIAH 55:8

It is with trepidation and distrust that most of us accept God's plan for our lives. The arrival of what we prayed so long for can be a bittersweet celebration. This long-awaited answer to our prayers acts more like an intruder—turning our plans inside out and our lives upside down. No wonder we don't feel hospitable and greet it with hisses and catcalls, keeping it at arms' length. As Martha Cory experienced, God's plan for our life may demand acquaintance with tough questions—*Is God trustworthy or not? And, if He is, do you trust Him with your life?*

Martha's story begins in her mid-twenties, when she made plans for the future. She envisioned marrying a tall, handsome man whom God would *soon* bring into her life—you did catch the word *soon!* She looked forward to being somebody's wife, mother, daughter-in-law, and neighbor, and she could hardly wait for the day that she and her future husband would present their parents with a grandchild. Martha never dreamed that:

- She would have to wait for a husband until she was thirty-three, and it would take them six years to conceive a child.
- Her mother would die of colon cancer before Martha's child was born, and her father would pass away the day she delivered her son, Nathaniel.
- Her father-in-law also would die and her mother-in-law would be in the later stages of senility by the time their grandson was born.

But the loss of these loved ones was not all that Martha mourned. She also grieved the loss of her son's normalcy. Nathaniel was born with Down's syndrome. Martha told God, "You made us wait and now this? Thanks a lot!" She talks about this period of time as one where she vacillated between "Don't even hint this child doesn't belong here!" to "Can't I have the child and let God take away the problems?"

A crucial moment came the evening Martha and her husband, Warren, shared a special maternity dinner on the roof of the hospital a few days after their son's birth. To Martha's surprise, Warren arrived dressed in the same rented tuxedo he had worn on their wedding day. It was his way of saying, "I am welcoming this child."

Three years after settling in with Nathaniel, Martha decided to conceive a second child, despite risks greater than 1 in 200 that the new baby would have Down's syndrome. "Warren and I decided the only reason not to do this would be if we didn't trust God," she said. At the end of her first trimester, they announced to the church choir where they are members—"Nathaniel wasn't quite what we expected, but we know that God didn't make a mistake. We want you to know that we trust God enough that whatever our second child is like, we'll receive it."

Six months later, they celebrated the arrival of a healthy boy—Timothy. During her pregnancy, Martha never anticipated that Timothy would be the one who would teach Nathaniel to walk. Today, when she looks at normal four-year-old Timothy helping seven-year-old Nathaniel, who is still in diapers and starting to make sentences, Martha thinks of Psalm 139 where it speaks of being fearfully and wonderfully made and says she is glad that God didn't put in a caveat *except for this group over here*. She admits that nothing will ever fill those holes in her life where grandparents could have been, but God has blessed her with "friends who take anything from me," prayer warriors, and a disability program at her church that provides a special helper who sits with Nathaniel during Sunday school and church.

Knowing that Nathaniel will never live a normal life, Martha knows she will spend the rest of her life "in a reworking process," but finds hope for the future when she sees other Down's syndrome children picking up toys. "I keep reminding myself that the same God who brought me Nathaniel brought me my parents, my husband, and Timothy," she says. "God sent us the babies meant for us. I can't imagine my life without them."

As we work through our own losses, trusting God will not come easy. When our plans go unfulfilled or our desires are unmet, we'll be tempted to say God is unfair, doesn't care, and can't be trusted. We will struggle to believe that he has something else in mind we can't yet imagine, let alone understand. But as Martha points out, we cannot have it both ways. Either we invite our Creator to do with our lives whatever He wants, whenever and for whatever purpose—or we don't. God never promised a fairy tale existence or a happily-ever-after ending, but He did promise His presence in the moment-to-moment living.

PRAYER PAUSE: *Lord, while I'm on my knees praying for Your will in my life and begging You to take back what you sent me, the thought never crosses my mind that my current situation could be part of Your plan. Help me not to miss the purpose You created me to fulfill and the unique message You are imparting in my heart. Remind me, as Your Word says, that planning my life isn't the problem; the hard part is letting You determine my steps (Proverbs 16:9).*

I would like to live . . . open to time and death painlessly, noticing everything, remembering nothing, choosing the given with a fierce and pointed will.

ANNIE DILLARD

My Mini Journal of Hope and Gratitude

I will repay you for the years the locust have eaten . . . JOEL 2:25 NIV

DATE	THE BEST PART OF ME THAT NO ONE SEES	TEN THINGS I WANT TO DO BEFORE I DIE

Trust God and keep your powder dry.

OLIVER CROMWELL

Who is this amazing woman?

- Her given name was Agnes Gonxha Bojaxhiu.
- She was born in 1910 in Skopje, Yugoslavia.
- She stood tall (although she was short) at only 4'11".
- In 1975, at 64, she said, "I'm getting old now," unaware she would live to be 87.
- She won the Nobel Peace Prize in 1979.
- By the mid-1990s, she had established 500 missions in 100 countries, from the hovels of third world nations to the ghettos of New York.
- Known for comforting the dying, she also celebrated life by setting up orphanages for unwanted babies and feeding the starving.[81]

ANSWER: MOTHER TERESA

Courageous Moments

When I Risk Hoping Again

Life is either a daring adventure or nothing at all.

HELEN KELLER

78. From this moment on . . .

I am overcome with joy because of your unfailing love, for you have seen my troubles, and you care about the anguish of my soul.

PSALM 31:7

Who says that roses can't bloom in December? Or that hope won't sprout in a broken heart? You and I know differently. We know that with God anything is possible—no matter how dark the moment or difficult the day.

From experience, you are discovering that whenever loss happens and whatever you lose, the healer of your heart and the lover of your soul is already on the job working on what concerns you. You are an example of a life going on after loss and growing beyond it.

This weekend my neighbor chattered about how short the days are getting *this time of year*, how she hates to let the flower beds go, and how hard it is to wait for spring; I nodded. I know. *So do you*. We know because we are doing just that. Sensing changes in the seasons of our lives. Struggling to let go of the past while anticipating what's ahead.

We know just how difficult it is to wait in hope when we can't see from here to there. That's why we keep repositioning ourselves for discovery because we know we are here for a purpose. Each time you and I stretch forward with a hopeful attitude and a vision of what God wants to do with the rest of our lives, we exercise faith. Each day is pregnant with moments that are life-giving and life-changing. Some days we can hardly wait for the new dream that is stirring in our heart to be born. And we dare ourselves to behave as though we believe it will.

In the meantime, we are trying to accept our limitations—emotional, mental, physical, and spiritual. We determine not to be afraid to cultivate more space for surprise and wonder. As we begin to make peace with change and expand with it, we realize we always had all the elasticity we needed. Because whatever happens, we are learning to say, "God and I will face this together." We know that loss has awakened us not only to our weakness and fears but to a strength greater than our own and a love broader than we thought. We can rely on a capacity much larger than ourselves, but we don't necessarily do so.

However, from this moment on, we keep trying to move out of our own way—keeping our hands empty, our hearts open, and our agendas flexible. We now know the importance of holding loosely whatever once defined us—people, possessions, and places. We will never forget how quickly those earthly props can be stripped away. Now we know that to live fully means to risk losing.

Although we each resist, loss is bringing about the purpose for which we were created—to glorify God with our lives while we find the deepest source of our identity in Him. His glory shines best through our moment-to-moment faithfulness. The more we keep coming back to that place where we see that God is all we *really* have, the more we realize He is all we need. Here, empty, open, and flexible are okay because God is enough.

PRAYER PAUSE: *Sovereign Lord, it is so hard to wait in hope for what I cannot see. I keep bumping into memories that remind me that a part of me has been taken away—a part I thought I could not live without. Help me remember that empty hands provide space for You to fill and an open heart means room for You to dwell. Give me courage to release my agenda and allow for the fullness of Your time and the working of Your will.*

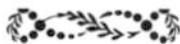

Only with winter patience
can we bring the deep-desired, long-awaited spring.

ANNE MORROW LINDBERGH

Note: *Anne Morrow Lindbergh (wife of pioneer aviator Charles Lindbergh) writes from experience. Her only son was kidnapped and murdered and Anne was widowed in 1974. Her best-known book is* Gift from the Sea.

79. *On my feet again*

Happy are those who are strong in the Lord,
who set their minds on a pilgrimage to Jerusalem. When they walk through
the Valley of Weeping, it will become a place of refreshing springs,
where pools of blessing collect after the rains!

PSALM 84:5, 6

It is said that a journey of a thousand miles begins with a single step. However, long-distance hikers say that the real journey begins before you even place one foot on the ground. Before a single step is taken, there must be commitment to the work ahead. The terrain visualized. Goals defined. Pride reined in. Doubts and fears corralled. Because it takes staying power to build the stamina needed to endure the stress and fatigue of the larger journey, lung capacity needs increasing. Muscles must strain, stretch, and strengthen. One's body, mind, emotions, and spirit must be brought into balance.

As would an athlete, you recognize the work that is needed. And you are pouring your passion into it. You are learning that you have to get your heart set before you get your feet wet. Each morning that you sling your feet off the bed, you are committing to the quest and building stamina to go the distance the day requires. You are also regaining your balance after months of destabilizing grief and unpredictable tears.

As a pilgrim who journeys a long distance to a sacred place, you are undertaking this moment-by-moment mission of faith. Instead of just putting your life on hold and waiting for the promised land, you are now trusting God in life's everydayness. You know that faith is more active get-up-and-at-it than passive wait-

and-see. It is exercised each time you rise above your circumstances—stretching in hope through the here-and-now while living with the end in mind. You practice faith when you strain past your fears.

Although you are well acquainted with the terror that comes with the territory, you are determined to get underway and maintain equilibrium. Experience has shown that being fearful and doubting yourself is the baggage we humans juggle as pilgrims in a foreign land. Now you aren't as quick to chide yourself when anxiety obscures the ground and envelopes your feet—and you swagger a little.

As you see yourself through this undulating terrain, you steel yourself to accept your apprehensions for what they are so you aren't thrown off center. You try to counterweight despair with hope and offset fear with courage. Instead of allowing pessimism and uncertainty to hold you down, you do your best to catch your misgivings early so you can swing into action again. You keep at it even when your heart quakes and the ground shakes.

You realize that being on your feet means the risk of falling down. Even when you tumble, you struggle to give yourself up to hope. You know that without hope, you will never take a single step to get the rest of your life's journey under way.

So with each new day, you grant yourself permission to start afresh. To trust God once more. To rediscover and depend on a strength that was there all along and always will be. To struggle to your feet and believe in yourself again.

In those rare moments when despair lifts, you catch sight of how far you have come. Your spirit soars. You are standing in sacred sky.

PRAYER PAUSE: *Oh, Father God, in this topsy-turvy world with its tedious everydayness, I tend to forget the larger journey and* *lose my balance. Now I see that faithfulness is what matters most. As You strengthen my faith for what lies ahead, remind me of the desires You have placed in my heart and renew my devotion to what you called me to do this moment in time. How I long to exercise hope every day of my life for the rest of my life!*

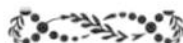

Set yourself earnestly to discover what you are made to do,
and then give yourself passionately to the doing of it.

MARTIN LUTHER KING, JR.

80. Standing tall

O Lord, you alone are my hope. I've trusted you, O Lord, from childhood. Yes, you have been with me from birth; from my mother's womb you have cared for me. No wonder I am always praising you!

PSALM 71:5, 6

You sense a shift in the wind and hear a rattle in the air. Just as the dry bones mentioned in Ezekiel stood up after being scattered across an ancient battlefield, you stand tall after your devastating loss (Ezekiel 37:1-14). You have come to life again despite long months of exposure to elements that can reduce trust to dust. Strained muscles and torn ligaments are healing and reattaching. Heart wounds are covering with wiser skin. Spiritual footing is strengthening. Parched hopes are being revived.

And you are giving life all you have. Nourishing your body. Getting enough sleep. Breathing slower. Laughing more.

You are holding your head high, thankful for the past and for God's presence while you grieve it. It is in the struggle that you are becoming stronger. You now know, however loss invades your life again, whether it trashes your trust, dries up your hopes, or batters your worth, your identity will remain secure in God.

As you shake off the sandy grains from your deepest valley, you see that God's thoughts toward you outnumber them (Psalm 139:17-18). He already knows all about those moments you wanted to die and the times you almost gave up, and He loves you anyway. You are accepted just as you are—weary and wobbly, but with the worn patina of a valuable piece of silver. As Archbishop William Temple explains, "My worth is what I am to God, and that is a marvelous great deal, for Christ died for *me*."[82]

With God's help, you are growing larger than your losses. You are rolling back those slumped shoulders because you are discovering that loss is not all of who you are. It's that way for Nicole. She had her innocence stolen by a rapist when she was nine. Though you might not share her history, you do share her commitment that life still has meaning and you will boldly live it out. Nicole wrote:

To the Person Who Raped Me

. . . You stole my innocence, that's true,
But there's something that you didn't do.
You didn't take my strength, you didn't take my heart.
You didn't take my faith in God,
Although in that you played a part.

. . . there's another thing you didn't take away from me.
You didn't take the gift I was meant to be.
My life was created for a purpose.
And just because you violated me,
Doesn't mean I'm worthless.[83]

PRAYER PAUSE: *Lord, thank you for bearing me up and for renewing my hope. Clothe me with your grace and mercy. Invigorate me with your life-giving breath. Stay beside me as I dare to stand my ground in the face of darkness and in the shadow of death. And when the terror of the unknown beats me down, may I release a fragrance pleasing to You, like the crushed lavender blossoms in my potpourri.*[84]

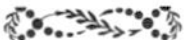

I feel safe in God's arms,
and I shall always be able to stand on my own two feet,
even when they are planted on the hardest soil of the harshest reality.

ETTY HILLESUM

81. Striding onward

Oh, that we might know the Lord! Let us press on to know him!
Then he will respond to us surely as the arrival of dawn
or the coming of rains in early spring.

HOSEA 6:3

There are many mountain climbers in the world but few were as determined as Norman Vaughn. He knew firsthand the physical difficulties that make climbing arduous—steep, slippery terrain and howling windstorms—and the emotional elements of discouragement and fear that conspire against such an onward, upward trek. In 1929, Vaughn was the dog handler for Admiral Byrd's expedition to the North Pole. He promised himself someday he would return to climb the mountain that was named after him.

He did, in 1994; but by this time he was eighty-nine, with a bad knee and a weak ankle. The thirty-degree slope he remembered turned out to be forty degrees. It would take him eight days to climb up; one day, down. But instead of being defeated, he decided to accept the challenge and let it push him. He also had help—7,129 footsteps were cut for him in the snow by fellow climbers so he could ascend Mount Vaughn.

In our trek through grief, that is what God does for us. He gives us courage and hope that there is some place left to go. We may not see the evidence of His footprints, but Jesus went before us. He is the way, and we are to follow in His steps (I Peter 2:21). However steep the terrain or deep the pit, we will pass securely.

I wondered if I would ever climb out of the pit I was in that first Christmas after my divorce. Since my daughter had chosen to visit her dad, I decided to travel to Israel with a group of her classmates and their parents. That trip remains one of the highlights of my life. New Year's Day we stopped for devotions in the hill country outside Jerusalem, just as the sun was coming up. Behind us was the bustling city, and far beyond our sight was the verdant Jordan Valley. I wedged myself between the rocks and thought about the words of Scripture—*hinds' feet on high places* (II Sam. 22:34; Hab. 3:19). One glance at the steep terrain below the roadway and I understood. Not only is the Holy Land one rugged rock after another, but if you needed a drink of river water, the way down is perpendicular. You would need sturdy legs, shoes with grip, and gutsy determination to traverse this treacherous terrain.

The landscape of grief is fraught with similar peril. It is more up, down, and all around than level and straight. We know how easy it is to make promises to ourselves, as Norman Vaughn did, and we know the difficulty of carrying them out. Sometimes it takes awhile for healing to get from our objective brain into our subjective heart. But to see the panoramic view, we must accept the risks that come with striding onward. Some days we struggle, others we can manage a good pace. What matters is not our speed or the distance covered but being faithful. One step at a time. One day at a time. One year at a time. Following Jesus.

PRAYER PAUSE: *Father, without weakness, how would I know Your strength. Without loss, how would I gain compassion for others. Without doubts, how would I know trust. Without fear, how would I know the price of courage. And how, without the struggle, would I learn to endure. Without Jesus, I would never find my way to You.*

Man cannot discover new oceans
until he has courage to lose sight of the shore.

UNKNOWN

82. Looking forward

For everything that was written in the past was written to teach us, so that through endurance and the encouragement of the Scriptures we might have hope.

ROMANS 15:4 NIV

Last evening I stepped out onto my deck to soak up the balmy Indian summer air, peek at stars, and enjoy the twinkling lights of distant and nearby cities. Our house could best be called "a work in progress," but on a clear night, the view is picture perfect and conducive to dreaming.

I thought about the first time that Richard and I stood on the deck before we moved in. We were exhausted from our work-week, a long, bumpy truck ride through traffic, and loading and unloading of boxes and furniture. We had been married less than a year and were looking forward to the day we would finally be settled into our home. That night I was filled with awe for much more than the obvious view. I had come so far from the dark days of my divorce, when I could not imagine myself surviving, let alone starting over a new life with such a wonderful man. I felt humbled and blessed, grateful that I had not allowed hope to die.

You, too, have come so far. You have traveled further that you ever imagined since those dark days in the tunnel. Here you are now—starting over after a time of endings, standing on the brink of a different season, looking forward to something new. Against the lingering chill of loss and the rapid gusts of change, the sky is clearing. You are pondering a vision of what God wants to do with your life six months, twelve months, and even five years from now, and you are daring yourself to behave as if you believe it.

Carolyn Hoffman did just that after her husband's sudden death from a heart attack. Hoping to carve out a new life for herself and successfully raise her daughter, Carolyn has journeyed far from the early days when she was so stunned she couldn't imagine taking on the responsibility of being a single parent and running the family business. She was determined to do things differently from her older sister, who upon being widowed, spent five years in her bedroom on Valium while her teenage son wandered the streets. "My sister's experience was like a crystal ball of what could happen unless I decided to do things differently," Carolyn says. "So when the down times came, I would think, 'I have two choices here—I can go to pieces like my sister or I can be strong and set an example for my daughter to follow.'" Today, Carolyn is a tour escort in Pennsylvania. Her daughter, only fourteen when her father died, will soon graduate from college.

When life goes up in smoke, it all comes down to hope. But it takes more than wishful thinking to behave like we believe what we hope for can happen. Hope requires a long view. Sometimes we hopefully wait. Other times we must hope against hope when a situation turns bleak. There are also times when we think all hope is gone.

One dark night, when Abraham thought his servants would have to be his heirs, God turned his attention to the sky and told him to count stars (Genesis 15). Abraham did. And although he made a few blunders along the way and was a hundred when Isaac was finally born, Romans 4:18 (NIV) says, "Against all hope, Abraham in hope believed and so became the father of many nations, just as it had been said to him, 'So shall your offspring be.'"

Both illusive and energizing, hope is sometimes all we have to cling to, fueling our will to go on. Hope is also grounded in God's promise of eternal life and His Word (Romans 15:4; Titus 1:2).

Without hope, our spirit withers and dies. Samuel Johnson said that remarriage is "the triumph of hope over experience." So is single-parenting or looking for your first job at midlife. Whenever you and I dare to do what we have never done before, hope prevails.

PRAYER PAUSE: *Lord of my life, I can't believe You have brought me this far. I stand before You with a mix of quiet astonishment and thundering delight. Show me the stars.*

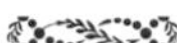

I will go anywhere, as long as it is forward.

DAVID LIVINGSTONE

83. Risking more

Now glory be to God! By his mighty power at work within us, he is able to accomplish infinitely more than we would ever dare to ask or hope.

EPHESIANS 3:20

If we are serious about starting a new life, we must lay ourselves open to the possibility of losing again. That does not mean we forget the deep loves of yesterday or their painful loss. It does mean we accept the risks of losing as part of living. Some of us are already placing ourselves into this adventure, and we are taking our chances. Others of us aren't so brave. We prefer sandbagging to being in what we perceive as harm's way.

Risk, by definition, is exposure to the possibility of injury or loss. It is akin to going to sea in a sieve or sailing too near the wind. Insurance companies base the cost of their policies on the risks taken. Scuba divers and pilots pay higher premiums than secretaries because their activities carry a higher risk.

A willingness to risk is what God asks of us. In the journey through grief, we have already taken a bold risk, because we cannot grieve what we have not lost, released, or watched die. Like a leap in the dark, we risked pain when we moved beyond denial. When we allowed doubts to rise to the surface, we unflinchingly laid our faith on the line. Each time we stepped into the unknown day, we took a chance that something might happen.

Now we must dare to trust and hope that we can continue the rest of the way. God never promised us a risk-free journey, only a safe arrival home. Believe me, I have looked for that verse in the Bible that says, "Go ahead and risk. All will turn out okay," only to discover the opposite. Ecclesiastes warns that there is risk to everything. Digging a well means we could fall in. Demolishing a wall could result in a snakebite. If we wait for any guarantees, we will never get anything done (Ecclesiastes 10:8-9; 11:4).

I asked a friend of mine, who is living with advanced prostate cancer, where he gets his courage. "I love life and fight for it," Cliff Coon says. "And I always ask for more from God—one more year, then another, because I understand each day is a gift. There's a good urgency about each day, but this urgency does not make me tense. It makes me realize that I should not waste my time."

God always calls us to love life—to fight for it. To make the most of each day. God said to Joshua, "Now that my servant Moses is dead, you must lead my people . . . I will not fail you or abandon you. Be strong and courageous." (Joshua 1:1-9).

God is calling us, as he called Joshua after he lost his mentor Moses, to fulfill the purpose for which He created us, and in the process, to lay ourselves open to the possibility of losing again. "Twenty years from now you will be more disappointed by the things you didn't do than by the ones you did," wrote Mark Twain. "So throw off the bowlines. Sail away from the safe harbor. Catch the trade winds in your sails. Explore. Dream. Discover."

PRAYER PAUSE: *Heavenly Father, intellectually I understand that security does not mean the absence of pain or danger, but Your presence in whatever I encounter. However, my heart won't let me forget the excruciating pain of losing those I've loved and so I hold back. Teach me to risk trusting You. Infuse me with courage and hope, so I can dive deeper and fly higher. I want to explore, to dream, and to discover Your purpose for the remaining days of my life.*

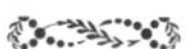

Oxygen is to the body what hope is to the soul.

EMIL BRUNNER

84. God, grant me courage to plant my hope in You!

. . . I will give her back her vineyards,
and will make the Valley of Achor [trouble] a door of hope.
There she will sing as in the days of her youth,
as in the day she came up out of Egypt.

HOSEA 2:15 NIV

"Tell me a story about one thing in your life that did not work out," Teresa Watkins said. We were talking about life in general and the specific topic of loss while she massaged my arm to stretch the tendons and increase blood supply to my carpal-tunnel-syndrome wrist.

I paused. "Well, I have to think about it," I said. "Maybe my divorce. Then, again, I learned a lot in the process, and I've moved on."

"That's the point!" she said.

In the weeks that followed, with each chapter I wrote, that conversation revisited me. It fed my thoughts while I pruned and fertilized my roses. I turned it over in my mind as I pulled weeds and spaded leaf mold into the stubborn clay of my flower beds. I now realize that its wisdom can be applied to my garden, my life, and this book.

We each have a life story—a story of love and loss. And its startling conclusion is this: It does work out—one way or the other. We do move on—one direction or another. That is what *living with losses of the heart* is all about.

Life's greatest lessons grow out of loss. We learn to reconcile our expectations with reality, and to let go. We learn to integrate who we are on the outside with who is on the inside, and to forgive those who hurt us. We learn to live with a sense of eternity instead of a sense of entitlement, and to trust God to work it all out. We learn that while we are longing to see our lives back in order, God is longing to show us himself. His unfailing love. His unchanging faithfulness. His beauty, goodness, and truth.

Cardinal John Henry Newman observed, "Growth is the only evidence of life." To create a life and a garden is to go in search of a better world, while we keep doing the mundane tasks of paying bills and pulling weeds. It is to allow loss to enlarge our hearts the way leaf mold enhances clay, while we nurture new life into being. It is to hope for a future we cannot see, while we live with that end in mind—whether it is a flower bouquet, a single moment without sorrow, or that heavenly day when God will make all things new (Revelation 21:4).[85] To create a life is to send our roots deep into God, while we bear in mind that things happen that can wipe out fields of lavender and years of dreams.

Now you know:

Loss is a risk you take for living and loving.
Anger, doubt, and fear mean you are human;
not that you are stuck.
There are angels in your midst and rainbows in the rain.
Empty is okay, because God is enough.
Hope requires a long view.
There is a future beyond grief.
You can dare to trust and hope again.

PRAYER PAUSE: *Creator God, I praise you for who You are. Without You, I cannot imagine a future—or a me in it. Thank you for rain that renews the sun-parched earth and for hope that restores my loss-ravaged heart. Now I understand that what happens within me* *is more important than what happens to me. Teach me how to plant my hope in You and to cultivate what matters—the eternal part that I will take with me when I leave the rest behind.*

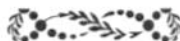

A new year can begin only because an old year ends.

MADELEINE L'ENGLE

My Mini Journal of Hope and Gratitude

For I know the plans I have for you . . .
to give you a future and a hope JEREMIAH 29:11

DATE	WHAT WORKED OUT THIS YEAR	MY VISION FOR NEXT YEAR

In the face of uncertainty, there's nothing wrong with hope.

HAFEZ

A Woman's Strength[86]

One day three men were walking along and came upon a raging river. They needed to get to the other side but had no idea how to do it. The first man prayed to God, saying, "Please, God, give me the *strength* to cross this river." Poof! God gave him big arms and strong legs, and he was able to swim across the river in about two hours.

The second man prayed to God, saying, "Please, God, give me the *strength and ability* to cross this river." Poof! God gave him a rowboat and he was able to row across the river in about three hours.

The third man had seen how this worked out for the other two, so he also prayed to God, saying, "Please, God, give me the *strength, ability, and intelligence* to cross this river." Poof! God turned him into a woman, who looked at the map, then walked across the bridge.

Topical Index

(ARRANGED BY CHAPTER NUMBERS)

Resource Index

CHRONIC ILLNESS:

Alzheimer's Association
919 N. Michigan Avenue, Suite 1100
Chicago, IL 60611
312-335-5813
800 272-3900
www.alz.org
e-mail: info@alz.org
Provides information and referral to local chapters

Alzheimer's Disease Education and Referral Center National Institute on Aging
P. O. Box 8250
Silver Spring, MD 20907-8250
800-438-4380
www.alzheimers.org
Provides information and referral

American Cancer Society (ACS)
1599 Clifton Road, N.E.
Atlanta, GA 30329
800-227-2345
www.cancer.org
Community-based voluntary health organization

American Institute for Cancer Research
P. O. Box 97167, Dept. U
Washington, DC 20090
800-843-8114
www.aicr.org
Provides information and referral, and Internet resources

Anxiety Disorders Association of America
1190 Parklawn Drive, Ste. 100
Rockville, MD 20852
301-231-9350
Provides information and referral

Make Today Count Mid-America Cancer Center
1235 E. Cherokee Street
Springfield, MO 65804
800-432-2273
National organization with local support groups

National Institute of Mental Health
5600 Fishers Lane, Rm. 7C-02
Rockville, MD 20857
888-8-ANXIETY
www.nimh.nih.gov
Provides information and referral

National Mental Health Association
1021 Price Street
Alexandria, VA 22314-2971
800-969-6642
www.nmha.org
Provides information and referral to local chapters

National Mental Health Services Knowledge Exchange Network
P. O. Box 4290
Washington, DC 20015
800-789-2647
www.mentalhealth.org
Provides information and Internet resources

National Multiple Sclerosis Society
733 Third Avenue
New York, NY 10017-3288
800-3434-4867
www.nmss.org
Information and referral to local chapters

Lutheran AIDS Network
Dr. Kristen Gebbie
Columbia School of Nursing,
Center of Health Policy
630 W. 108th Street, Ste. 6
New York, NY 10032
212-305-1794
Information and referral

Lutheran Services in America
2177 Youngman Avenue
St. Paul, MN 55116
800-664-3848
www.lutheranservices.org
Social ministry organization

National Hospice and Palliative Care Organization
1700 Diagonal Road, Ste. 300
Alexandria, VA 22314
800-658-8898 (for hotline)
703-243-5900
www.nhpco.org
Provides information and referral to local programs

SUDDEN DEATH (ACCIDENTAL AND NATURAL):

Mothers Against Drunk Driving (MADD)
511 E. John Carpenter

Freeway, #700
Irving, TX 75062
214-744-MADD (for general information)
800-GET-MADD (for victims)
www.madd.org
Information and referral to local chapters

DEATH OF A CHILD:

Alive Alone
11115 Dull Robinson Road
Van Wert, OH 45891
419-238-1091
e-mail: alivalone@bright.net
Self-help network providing information to bereaved parents

BASIS for Bereaved Parents and Families
237 Fairfield Avenue
Upper Darby, PA 19082
610-352-7177
Provides information and referral

Bereaved Parents of the USA
P. O. Box 95
Park Forest, IL 60466
630-971-3490
www.bereavedparentsusa.org
Provides information and referral

Sudden Infant Death Syndrome Alliance (SIDS)
1314 Bedford Avenue, Ste. 210
Baltimore, MD 21208
410-653-8226 (for general information)
800-221-7437 (for hotline)
www.sidsalliance.org
Not-for-profit voluntary health organization; information and referral

Parents of Murdered Children, Inc.
100 E. 8th Street, Ste. B-41
Cincinnati, OH 45202
513-721-5683
888-818-PMC
www.pome.com
Emotional support and information for survivors

The Compassionate Friends
P. O. Box 3696
Oak Brook, IL 60522-3696
630-990-0010
www.compassionate-friends.org
Information and referral to local chapters

SUICIDE:

American Association of Suicidology
4201 Connecticut Avenue, NW, Ste 408
Washington, DC 20008
202-237-2280
www.suicidology.org
Not-for-profit organization provides information

Suicide Prevention Advocacy Network (SPANUSA)
5034 Odin's Way
Marietta, GA 30068
888-649-1366
e-mail: act@spanusa.org
www.spanusa.org
Provides information and referral

Lifekeeper Foundation
Sandy Martin, Founder
3740 Crestcliff Court
Tucker, GA 30084
678-937-9297
e-mail: lifekeeper@aol.com
www.lifekeeper@aol.com
Provides information and referral

Suicide Awareness—Voices of Education (SA/VE)
P. O. Box 24507
Minneapolis, MN 55424
612-946-7998
www.save.org
Provides information and referral

Comforting Friends
P. O. Box 214463
Sacramento, CA 95821
916-392-0664
An outreach program of Survivors of Suicides, information and referrals

Suicide Bereavement Support
2116 NE 18th
Portland, OR 97212
503-699-8103
Provides information and referral

GRIEF SUPPORT AND INFORMATION:

AARP Widowed Persons Service
601 E. Street, NW
Washington, DC 20049
202-434-2260
www.aarp.org/griefandloss
Provides information and referral to support groups

Bereavement Publishing, Inc.
5125 N. Union Blvd, Ste. 4
Colorado Springs, CO 80918
888-604-4673
www.bereavementmag.com
Provides information

Divorce Care
P.O. Box 1739
Wake Forest, NC 27588
800-489-7788
wwwdivorcecare.org
Provides information and referral to local support groups.

GriefNet
e-mail:
griefnet@griefnet.org
www.griefnet.org
Provides Internet library, newsletter, and e-mail-based support groups

PastoreCare
Dr. Bert Moore, Jr.
Executive Director
P.O. Box 52044
Raleigh, NC 27612
919-787-7024
e-mail: pstrcare@concentric.net
www.pastorcare.org
Provides ongoing counseling for pastors' wives or ex-pastors' wives

WEBSITES RESOURCES (WWW)

All About Hospice
hospice-america.org

American Cancer Society
cancer.org

American Medical Association—Women's Health
ama.assn.org

American Menopause Association
menopause.org

American Parkinson Disease Association, Inc.
apdaparkinson.com

Center for Disease Control and Prevention
cdc.gov/od/owh/whhome.htm

Center for Lymphoma—Hodgkin and non-Hodgkin
cfl.org

Cerebral Palsy Support Network
cpsn.21stcentury.com

Cystic Fibrosis Foundation
cff.org

Disability Outreach of Joni Eareckson Tada
jafministries.com

Family Caregiver Alliance
caregiver.org

Healthfinder
healthfinder.gov

Hospice Foundation of America
hospicefoundation.org

International Association of Cystic Fibrosis Adults
iacfa.com

JAMA Women's Health Information Center
ama-assn.org/special/womh/womh.htm

Legal Services Network (AARP)
aarp.org/lsn

Mayo Clinic Women's Health Center
mayohealth.org/mayo/common/htm/womenpg.htm

Multiple Sclerosis Society
mssociety.org

Muscular Dystrophy Association
mdausa.org

National Alliance of Breast Cancer Organizations
nabco.org

National Association for Continence
nafc.org

National Family Caregivers Association
nfcacares.org

National Federation of Interfaith Volunteer Caregivers
nifivc.org

National Hospice and Palliative Care Organization
nhpco.org

National Mental Health Association
nmha.org

National Network of Libraries of Medicine
nnlm.nlm.nih.gov

National Women's Health Resource Center
healthywomen.org

National Osteoporosis Foundation
nof.org

New York Times Women's Health Site
nytimes.com/specials/women

Supportive Care of the Dying
careofdying.org

The Partnership for Caring
partnershipforcaring.org

The Women's Cancer Network Site
wcn.org

Endnotes

1 Lavender has been used since Roman times for its antiseptic, cleansing, and healing qualities, and its ability to deter insects. In the Bible, lavender was known as spikenard. John 12:3, 5, refers to the costly ointment made from this aromatic herb. Mary's offering equaled a day's wages. "A dinner was prepared in Jesus' honor. Martha served and Lazarus sat at the table with him. Then Mary took a twelve-ounce jar of expensive perfume made from the essence of nard, and she anointed Jesus' feet with it and wiped his feet with her hair. And the house was filled with fragrance." (John 12:2-3)

2 Gaby Wood, London Observer Service, "Here's almost everything you ever wanted to know about chocolate," *The Daily Review,* August 7, 1996, C-5; "Chocolate is good for heart," *The Daily Review,* date unknown, A-1.

3 Jennifer Reid Holman, "Foods that boost your moods," *Ladies Home Journal,* November 1995, p. 156.

4 Joni Eareckson Tada, *Glorious Intruder* (Portland: Multnomah, 1989), p. 142.

5 *The Wycliffe Bible Dictionary* (Chicago: Moody Press, 1975), p. 1104.

6 Associate Press, "Heart transplanted from baby without a brain," *The Daily Review,* January 31, 1998, A-12.

7 Richard A. Swensen, M.D., *Margin: Restoring Emotional, Physical, Financial, and Time Reserves to Overloaded Lives* (Colorado Springs, Colo.: NavPress, 1992), p. 100.

8 James 4:15 NASB

9 Luke 22:42

10 Nuna Alberts, "The Healing Power of Sleep," *Good Housekeeping*, March 2000, p. 158.

11 Psalm 139:17-18

12 "Let go. Cease striving. I [God] will make it happen," Psalm 46: 10 NASB (Open Expanded Edition)

13 Hebrews 11:1: "What is faith? It is the confident assurance that what we hope for is going to happen. It is the evidence of things we cannot yet see."

14 Job 13:13-17; Psalm 42:5, 9, 11; 43:5; Mark 15:33-34; John 9:1-41; 11:1-44

15 "Teenage Suicide—the Silent Threat," an A&E Television Home Video that aired on "Investigative Reports" in 1999. Features Trish and Alan Schuster's story of their daughter, Dawn (see Chapter 12). Available at New Video Group, 126 Fifth Avenue, New York, NY 10011.

16 Philip Yancey, *Disappointment With God* (Grand Rapids, Mich.: Zondervan, 1988), pp. 201, 200.

17 Editors of Sunset Books and *Sunset* Magazine, *Cactus & Succulents* (Menlo Park, Calif.: Lane Publishing, 1978), p. 35.

18 "Singing cheerful songs to a person whose heart is heavy is as bad as stealing someone's jacket in cold weather or rubbing salt in a wound." Proverbs 25:20

19 Philip Yancey, *Disappointment With God* (Grand Rapids, Mich.: Zondervan, 1998), p. 207.

20 Psalm 146:1-2

21 Marilyn Elias, "We're sick of being stressed out," *USA Today,* May 4, 2000, p. 8D.

22 Kathleen Fackelmann, "The power of prayer," USA Today, July 18, 2000, p. 7D.

23 David Hazard, *Majestic Is Your Name* (Minneapolis, Minn.: Bethany House,

1993), pp. 11-13, 86. This is Hazard's paraphrase of *The Life of Theresa of Jesus.*

24 Archibald Hart, *Growing Up Divorced* (Ann Arbor, Mich.: Vine Books, 1991), pp. 160, 32.

25 Richard Willing, "Twister's true cost revealed day by day," *USA Today,* May 3, 2000, pp. 17-18A.

26 Nina Shengold, "Home Is Where the Heart Is," *Living Fit,* January/February 1997, p. 126.

27 Gerald Sittser, *A Grace Disguised* (Grand Rapids, Mich.: Zondervan, 1996), p. 36.

28 Ibid, p. 18.

29 Ibid, p. 43.

30 Sharon Randall, "Love and loneliness," *The Daily Review*, March 18, 2000, p. L-7.

31 Jim Smoke, *Your World Right Side Up* (Colorado Springs, Colo.: Focus on the Family, 1995), p. 85.

32 "Faith is the *substance of things hoped for*, the *evidence of things not seen.*" Hebrews 11:1 KJV (italics mine)

33 Linda L. Snyderman, *Necessary Journeys* (N.Y.: Hyperion, 2000), p. 1.

34 Cathy Hainer, "In effect, I am a virtual prisoner in my body," *USA Today,* December 6, 1999, p. 9D.

35 "The Lord is my rock and my fortress and my deliverer." Psalm 18:2 NASB

36 Job 33:15-17

37 Excerpted from Catherine Marshall's poem, "Give Me A Dream."

38 Bob George, *Classic Christianity* (Eugene, Ore.: Harvest House,1989), pp. 83, 84.

39 Maureen Boland, "Worried Sick? Don't Let Anxiety Harm Your Health," *Family Circle,* April 22, 1997, p.76.

40 Dean Ornish, M.D., *Love and Survival* (N.Y.: HarperCollins, 1998), p. 192.

41 Words by Civilla D. Martin, 1905. Tune, GOD CARES, by W. Stillman Martin, 1905.

42 Submitted by Judy Ralph, Burlington, Ontario, Canada.

43 Dr. Charles Stanley, *How to Handle Adversity* (Nashville, Tenn.: Thomas Nelson, 1989), p. 71.

44 Gerald Sittser, *A Grace Disguised* (Grand Rapids: Minn.: Zondervan, 1996), p. 87.

45 John P. Splinter, *The Complete Divorce Recovery Handbook* (Grand Rapids, Minn.: Zondervan, 1992), p. 110.

46 Lewis Smedes, *The Art of Forgiving* (N.Y.: Random House, 1996), p. 167.

47 "Private Life and Public Morality," *Citizen,* a publication of Focus on the Family, November 1998, p. 6.

48 "Social support is defined as information leading the subject to believe that he is cared for and loved, esteemed, and a member of a network of mutual obligations." "Emotional support involves the verbal and nonverbal communication of caring and concern—that you are valued and loved and have the opportunity for intimacy."(From *Love & Survival,* pp. 28, 29)

49 Peggy Noonan, "Looking Forward: Why We Need Girl Talk," *Good Housekeeping,* February 2000, p. 176.

50 Karen Peterson, "To fight stress, women talk, men walk," *USA Today,* August 7, 2000, p. D1.

51 *Love & Survival,* p. 13.

52 Genesis 18:2-8; Luke 15:10; Hebrews 1:14; I Peter 1:12

53 Genesis 24:7, 40; I Kings 19:5-8; Psalm 34:7; Daniel 6:22; Acts 8:26; 27:23, 24; I Peter 1:12

54 Genesis 21:17-19; Judges 13:2-21; I Kings 19:5-7; I Chronicles 21:16-18; Matthew 28:2; John 20:12-13

55 Dr. Billy Graham, *Angels: God's Secret Agents* (N.Y.: Doubleday, 1975), pp. 87, 100.

56 Deborah Blum, "Finding Strength," *Psychology Today,* May/June 1998, p. 67.

57 Philip Yancey, *The Jesus I Never Knew*

(Grand Rapids, Mich.: Zondervan, 1995), p. 266, 267.

58 Ibid, p. 273.

59 Ibid, p. 275.

60 Ibid. p. 275.

61 Joni Eareckson Tada, *JAF Newsletter*, December year unknown, p. 3.

62 Kari West, "The State of Affairs," *The Plain Truth Magazine*, July/August 2000, p. 37.

63 Psalm 59:9-10; Mark 13:31; Hebrews 1:12; 13:8

64 Oswald Chambers, *My Utmost for His Highest* (Grand Rapids, Mich: Discovery House Publishers, 1992), May 20 selection.

65 Lawrence O. Richards, *Expository Dictionary of Bible Words* (Grand Rapids, Mich.: Zondervan, 1985), p. 189; Charles F. Pfeiffer, et al, *The Wycliffe Bible Encyclopedia A-J* (Chicago: Moody Press, 1975), p. 377.

66 Paul J. Achtemeier, gen. ed., *Harpers Bible Dictionary* (New York: Harper & Row, 1985), p. 851; Charles F. Pfeiffer, et al, ed., *The Wycliffe Bible Encyclopedia* (Chicago: Moody Press, 1975), p. 271.

67 Submitted by Renee Trudell; quotation from Internet, author unknown. The name *Amber* was added.

68 Lewis Smedes, *The Art of Forgiving* (New York: Random House, 1996), p. 174.

69 Donna Brown Hogarty, "And the Good News Is...," *Ladies Home Journal*, December 1993, p. 116.

70 Jill Gerston, "Lady of living Martha Stewart doesn't waste any time," *The Daily Review*, October 25, 1994, p. C-4.

71 Hebrew for "four liters" or "two quarts."

72 "For we through the Spirit, by faith, are waiting for the hope of righteousness." Galatians 5:5 NASB

73 Philip Yancey, *Where Is God When It Hurts?* (Grand Rapids, Mich.: Zondervan, 1990), p. 207.

74 Third verse of "I Sing the Mighty Power of God," written in 1784 by Isaac Watts; music by Gesangbuch der Herzogl, Wuttenberg, Germany.

75 Richard Foster, *Celebration of Discipline* (San Francisco: HarperSan Francisco, 1878), pp. 87-89.

76 Kerry Walters, *Godlust—Facing the Demonic, Embracing the Divine* (Mahwah, N.J.: Paulist Press, 1999), p. 93.

77 Jeanne Satre, *Eight Was Not Enough* (Phoenix, Ariz.: ACW Press, 1998).

78 Condensed from *Kaiser Permanente's Senior Outlook*, Fall 1999, p. 10.

79 From *Kaiser Permanente K-Plus Fitness* flier, no date or page number. (Note on flier indicates: Excerpts from *Healthy Pleasures* by Robert Ornstein and David Sobel.)

80 Alison Stein Wellner and David Adox, "Happy Days," *Psychology Today*, May/June 2000, pp. 36, 35.

81 Dan Wooding, *Your Poverty Is Greater Than Ours*. From an online transmission from ASSIST.

82 Citizen and Churchman, Eyre and Spottiswoode, 1941, p. 74. Italics mine.

83 Excerpt from "To the Person Who Raped Me," ©2000 Nicole.

84 The genus *Lavandula* is an ornamental herb native to southern Europe and the Mediterranean. These sun-loving plants thrive in hot weather, tolerate a wide range of soils as long as they are well-drained, and require two to three growing seasons to reach a mature size. Grown for oil and showy flowers, lavender is also dried for use in potpourri, sachets, and wands.

85 "There will be no more death or mourning or crying or pain, for the old order of things has passed away." Revelation 21:4 NIV

86 Title mine; source is an e-mail forwarded from Sharon Jones.

More than just entertain, Cook Communications Ministries hopes to inspire you to fulfill the great commandment: to love God with all your heart, soul, mind, and strength; and your neighbor as yourself. Towards that end, the author wishes to share these personal thoughts.

Heart

More than anything else, loss continues to teach me about myself, life, and God. I am learning not to beat myself up for loving and trusting. When my first marriage unexpectedly ended, I vowed not to love or trust anyone else again. Initially, I looked upon love and trust as my faults, not my gifts. Now, I realize that they are who I am at the core of my being—character qualities patterned after God's own heart. I am also learning that once I get to heaven, my heavenly Father won't scan my chest for a badge that reads, "Perfectly Healthy, Happy Life." Instead, He will look at my heart to see if I have been faithful to Him through it all.

Soul

Perhaps you struggle believing that God really cares or is in control. I struggle with that, too! Loss can easily shake our spiritual foundation in this fallen, fickle world where loved ones get sick and die, and not everyone keeps a promise. But the incredible paradox is this: As we grieve, we want to see our lives back in order, while God wants to show us Himself. "But the Lord is faithful; he will make you strong and guard you from the evil one. . . . May the Lord bring you into an even deeper understanding of the love of God and the endurance that comes from Christ" (II Thessalonians 3:3, 5).

Mind

Several authors have inspired and encouraged me along the way. I've tried to share some of their insights in this book, so you might decide to use the book's endnotes as a reading list. I also recommend reading Proverbs, Ecclesiastes, and Jeremiah's thoughts on trust and hope (Jeremiah 17:5-8; 29:11) in the New Living Translation. If you liked *Dare to Trust, Dare to Hope Again* and are going through a divorce, you may be interested in reading *When He Leaves,* or in receiving the free *DivorceWise Newsletter.* Additional information and inspiration can be found on my website:
www.gardenglories.com, or by writing me at P. O. Box 11692, Pleasanton, CA 94588 or kariwest@juno.com for e-mail.

Strength

Trust. Hope. These are not pie-in-the-sky concepts for the fainthearted, but dauntless words. They evoke a spirit of daring that provokes me to believe that with my confidence in God I really can sling my feet off the bed and into the unknown day—whatever happens. My prayer is that this book will encourage you to believe that you can do that, too! Yes, I still battle the tendency to pull the covers over my head to make the world go away, but I have discovered that my Creator has His eye on me—and on you. He already knows our thoughts, understands our situation, loves us passionately, and graces us with tomorrow to start again.

Father God: In this very hour, enfold this reader in Your arms of mercy. Settle her thoughts and calm her fears. Provide rest. May she feel secure, affirmed, and loved. Don't let her tears blind her to the possibility of new life springing from her parched hopes, shattered dreams, or tarnished memories. Clear a path for her out of the wilderness of grief. As she digs her faith deep into You, may her despair give way to a living hope—a future she cannot yet imagine and a deeper, more authentic relationship with You than she ever expected. Amen.

Kari West